Circle Time Activities

Carson-Dellosa Publishing LLC
Greensboro, North Carolina

Note that some activities in this book may present safety issues. Before beginning the activities, ask families' permission and inquire about the following:
- Children's food allergies and religious or other food restrictions
- Possible latex allergies
- Children's scent sensitivities and/or allergies
- Children's plant and animal allergies

Also remember:
- Uninflated or popped balloons may present a choking hazard.
- Magnets and small pieces containing magnets should be kept away from young children who might mistakenly or intentionally swallow them. Seek immediate medical attention if you suspect a child may have swallowed a magnet.
- Exercise activities may require adult supervision. Children should always warm up prior to beginning any exercise activity and should stop immediately if they feel any discomfort during exercise.
- All children's families are different. Before beginning any family activity, review the activity cards and remove any that could cause sensitivity issues.
- Never leave students unattended around a hot lamp. Touching a hot lightbulb can cause burns.
- Keep boiling water away from students.

Credits

Content Editor: Joanie Oliphant

Copy Editor: Julie B. Killian

Layout Design: Lori Jackson

Carson-Dellosa Publishing LLC
PO Box 35665
Greensboro, NC 27425 USA
www.carsondellosa.com

ISBN 978-1-936024-83-4
06-252197784

Table of Contents

Introduction

Circle time is an important part of an early childhood program. Circle time gives young children an opportunity to learn how to be a part of a group, develop listening skills, experience music and movement, and play games. Circle time also provides opportunities for exploring new concepts and practicing social skills such as sharing and cooperating. Other benefits include enhanced levels of self-confidence, improved communication skills, and working together to build a caring community of learners.

Circle Time Activities is divided into four chapters, each reflecting an early childhood curriculum area based on Early Learning Standards set forth by the National Association for the Education of Young Children (NAEYC). The activities included foster young children's social-emotional development, language and literacy skills, and understanding of math and science concepts. In addition, music and movement activities are included to strengthen fine and gross motor skills, and activities for creative arts will inspire creativity and imaginative play. The Concept and Activity Matrix on pages 7–9 identify specific activities that focus on preferred classroom themes and concepts.

Starting the Year

At the beginning of the school year, establish ground rules for circle time. Write the rules on a sign and attach pictures showing each rule. Gently remind children who forget the rules by pointing to the appropriate picture. Sometimes, a silly gesture or sound can be more effective than words and will get attention more quickly. Examples of circle time rules are to sit quietly, listen when others are speaking, wait your turn, and speak one at a time.

Establishing a circle time routine is essential. It is much easier to introduce new topics and concepts within a familiar framework. Give children ample notice before circle time begins. Established rules, such as whether interrupted projects should be left out or put away, will help children comfortably transition from their current project to enter the circle. At the beginning of the school year, younger children have a short attention span, which is usually not more than four or five minutes per activity, and no more than two to three activities per circle time. Older children are more able to stay engaged for longer periods of time but will still get restless after 15 minutes or so. Many activities can be started in the circle and completed in the open classroom. Extensions of circle time are also possible, such as an art project or a learning center project that relates to a circle time activity.

Making the Most of Circle Time

Encourage everyone to join in circle time with the understanding that some children take longer than others to be comfortable as active participants in a group. With time and encouragement, most children will begin to participate. Circle time should be a time of sharing and trust. Help children feel secure by seating the ones closest who need the most encouragement and never allow children to make fun of a mistake.

Invite children to circle time by getting their attention. Softly beat a tom-tom, shake a tambourine, or sing a short song. Repeat until everyone has gathered. Encourage those who arrive first to join in.

Children enjoy repetition and predictability. Predictable patterns and events help them feel secure. Change the method or song used about once per month. A suggested song is "Get Ready for Circle Time," sung to the tune of "The Farmer in the Dell."

> Get ready for circle time,
>
> Get ready for circle time,
>
> Hi, ho, it's time you know,
>
> Get ready for circle time.

When children are reluctant to join the circle, try this song, sung to the tune of "Way Down Yonder in the Paw Paw Patch."

> Where oh where is our friend…(name)?
>
> Where oh where is our friend…(name)?
>
> Where oh where is our friend…(name)?
>
> Please join us at our circle time.

Starting circle time by reading a favorite book also helps children settle down. Children enjoy reading books over and over. Always read a book in advance before using it for circle time to make certain it is appropriate for the children. A lack of comfort with the words, pictures, or concepts will be noticeable and distracting to children. Follow a pattern such as read a story, opening activity, song or finger play, and closing activity. Once a pattern is established, aim for variety. Songs and finger plays can be quiet or loud and can involve a lot of movement or none. Stories can be told with big books, puppets, or a flannel board; props and games can run the gamut from beanbag tosses to relays. Keep circle time activities fresh and interesting. If children begin to lose interest, switch to a different activity. Whether the objective is to introduce a new concept or review what children have already learned, keep it simple and keep it short. Above all, have fun!

Daily Business

Circle time can be viewed as the "morning meeting" of the preschool day. Here are some suggested "business" matters to include:

Weather

You can approach the subject of weather in many interesting ways: Have the weather helper dress a stuffed animal in the appropriate clothing for the day or invite the weather person to place appropriate weather stickers on the class calendar. Create or purchase charts for displaying weather categories.

Helpers

At circle time, discuss the jobs that need to be done around the classroom. Create enough jobs so that every child has some responsibility each day. In addition to the line leader, weather helper, and snack helpers, assign children to be greeters, energy savers, song selectors, and first aid helpers.

Song/Finger Play Board

Using a colorful board, draw or find pictures to illustrate favorite class songs and finger plays. Invite the song selector to point to and choose the songs and finger plays used that day in circle time.

Calendar

Children enjoy songs and finger plays that reinforce the days of the week and the months of the year. Have the calendar helper point to or turn over the current day's date on the calendar and sing it to the group. This is also a good time of day to discuss routines, ("We always have music class on Mondays"), lunch menus ("Thursday is chicken day"), or special events ("Tomorrow we will be visiting the grocery store").

Super Stretches

After all of the "business" is taken care of in circle time, children will be ready for a good, long s-t-r-e-t-c-h. Here's an example:

I stand on tiptoe like a crane.	*Stand on tiptoes and stretch arms up.*
I stretch my wings out like a plane.	*Spread arms out to sides.*
I lean to the sides like a crescent moon.	*Arms over head, hands touch, lean left, then right.*
I bend 'til my back is as round as a balloon.	*Bend over and try to touch toes.*
I stand up straight, as straight as can be.	*Stand up, arms at sides.*
I am so glad that I am me.	*Wrap arms around self and hug.*

Concept and Activity Matrix

A = Social Emotional Development
B = Language and Literacy
C = Math

D = Science
E = Physical Development
F = Creative Arts

Activity	Page	A	B	C	D	E	F
1-2-3-4-5	70					•	
A Magic Plant	57				•		
A-A-R-G-H!	17	•				•	
Alive vs. Not Alive	66		•		•		
All About Me	117, 126–129					•	•
Animals	142–144				•	•	
Animal Switch	90				•	•	
Animal Walks	71				•	•	
Apples	118					•	•
Applesauce	84				•	•	
Are You My Mother?	38		•				
Awesome Animals	60				•		
Baby Games	98		•		•		
Balance Beam Color Land	83					•	
Balance Beam Skills	83					•	
Ball Butting	79				•	•	
Beanbag Games	23, 24					•	
Bear Cave Hide	72				•	•	
Bears in Chairs	54		•	•		•	
Bell Stories	106		•			•	
Birdseed Math	50		•	•			
Block Bonanza	49			•			
A Box of Circles	44			•			
Brick Building Mural	152						•
Bubble Wrap Play	93				•	•	
Build a Tower	96					•	•
The Bunny Hop	73				•	•	
Bunny Number Hop	72			•		•	
Cat Warm-up	75				•	•	
Caterpillar to Butterfly	155				•		•
Cattle Call	77				•	•	
Chalk It Up	154					•	•
Changes	37	•	•				
Chicken, Chicken, Who Has Your Egg?	79				•	•	
Chocolate Chip Cookie Count	45			•		•	
Cinderella Shoe Match	27	•				•	
The Circle of Noise	21	•				•	•
Clapping Around	110					•	•
Cobra Stretches	78				•	•	
Color Code Game	104			•		•	•

Activity	Page	A	B	C	D	E	F
Color Run	54			•		•	
Color Square Dance	105			•		•	•
Colorful Eggs	94				•	•	
Community	149	•				•	•
Comparing Rocks	66		•		•		
Concept Circle Game	29		•			•	
Counting	130–132					•	•
Counting Catches	41			•		•	
Counting Song	43		•	•			
Dinosaur Bone Drop	98					•	
Dinosaurs	124					•	•
Dot-to-Dot Mural	99					•	•
Drumbeat Movement	108					•	•
Drumstick Hunt	107					•	•
The Duck Family	74		•				
Duck Waddle Relay Race	74				•	•	
Earthworms	160					•	•
Emotions Die Roll	17	•				•	
Everyone Needs a Home	58				•		
Fabric Lotto	32		•	•			•
Fabric Matching	48			•			
Farm Animals	119					•	
Farmer in the Dell	159		•			•	
Favorite Pets	76				•	•	
The Feather Dance	92					•	•
Find Your Partner	75					•	
Fish in the Sea	103		•		•	•	
Flashlight, Flashlight, Where Are You?	91				•	•	
Floating Fish	67				•		
Fly or Run?	31		•			•	
Follow the Leader	70					•	
Footprints	68			•		•	
Footprints Frenzy	50						
Friendship Quilt	15	•					•
Froggy Freeze	112					•	•
Greetings from Around the World	27	•	•				
Group Sit	88					•	
Group Weave	88			•		•	
Habitat Game	58				•		•
Hand Harmonies	100					•	•
Happy Hands, Sad Hands	16	•					

Concept and Activity Matrix

A = Social Emotional Development
B = Language and Literacy
C = Math

D = Science
E = Physical Development
F = Creative Arts

Activity	Page	A	B	C	D	E	F
Hide and Tell	51		•	•		•	
Hoops of Fun	80		•			•	
Hop Like the Animals	73				•	•	
Hop on Colors	54			•		•	
Hopping Races	98					•	
Hot Potato	86					•	•
How Do Plants Grow?	57				•		
How Many Ways?	34		•				
How Many?	40		•	•			•
How We Travel	150					•	•
I Am a Tree	33		•			•	
I'm a Special Person	151	•					•
I Am Not Afraid of Monsters	36	•	•				
I'm Thinking	30		•				
Ice Pass	99				•	•	
If You Were a Carpenter	26	•					•
Imagination Nature Walk	21	•	•				
The Ins and Outs of Circles	42			•		•	
Juggling	87					•	
Jumping the Brook	70				•	•	
Just Fruity	89					•	
Ladder on the Floor	92					•	
Learning the Ropes	69					•	
Let's Talk About Honesty	35	•	•				
Letter Basket	31		•				
Light Show	64				•		
Listening for Pitch	111					•	•
Little Birds	74					•	
Lizards Inside, Dinosaurs Outside	22	•	•				
London Bridge	103					•	•
Loud and Soft Sounds	65				•		•
Magnets	66				•		
Make It Pop	102			•			•
Make Stories Live	29		•				•
Making Dolls Dance	67				•		
Making a Cloud	57				•		
Marching Band Parade	113					•	•
Mashed Potatoes	84					•	
The Mirror and Me	11	•					•
Mitten Match	97			•		•	
Mother Goose Activities	158		•			•	

Activity	Page	A	B	C	D	E	F
Moving Like Animals	71				•	•	
Moving with Carpet Squares	81					•	
Music Detectives	112					•	•
Musical Chairs and More	101	•				•	•
Musical Echoes	112		•			•	•
My Bandage Story	29		•				
My House	30		•	•			
Name Chant	107	•	•	•		•	•
Name Clap	110	•				•	•
Name Game	10	•	•			•	
Nature Mural	154					•	•
No-Lose Duck, Duck, Goose	94				•	•	
Number Match Game	41			•			
Nursery Rhyme Fun	157	•	•			•	•
Nutrition	125					•	•
Obstacle Course	91					•	
Ocean	120					•	•
One, Two, Pick Up Sticks	43			•			
Outdoor Circle Time	13	•					•
Over and Under	87			•		•	
Over and Under the Bridge	42			•		•	
Pancake Stretches	102		•			•	
Paper Trail	85					•	
Parachute Fun	82	•	•			•	
Partner Jive	100					•	•
Pass on a Hand Hug	10	•					
People, Places, and Things	55		•		•		
Percussion Instruments	113					•	•
Pets	145, 146				•	•	•
Picnic Lunch	89				•	•	
Poof Ball Toss	51			•		•	
A Pretty Plant	57				•		
Properties	64		•		•		
Puddles	95				•	•	
Pumpkin Patch	159					•	•
Questions, Questions	33		•				
Quiet Countdown	22	•	•				
Rhyming Riddles	34		•				
Rhythm Time	109					•	•
Rocking Horses	75					•	

Concept and Activity Matrix

A = Social Emotional Development
B = Language and Literacy
C = Math
D = Science
E = Physical Development
F = Creative Arts

Activity	Page	A	B	C	D	E	F
Roll-A-Ball	71					•	
Rough or Smooth?	65		•		•		
Row Your Boat	156					•	•
Sandwich Squish	104	•			•		
Seashell Sorting	49		•	•			
Seasonal Charades	97				•	•	
Sharing Fair	25	•					
Show Me Your Favorite Color	13	•	•				
Simon Says	11	•				•	
Six Little Ducks	114	•				•	•
Slippery Fish	77				•	•	
Snake in a Tunnel	78					•	
Sorting Circles	44			•	•		
Sorting Hard and Soft	65				•		
Sponge Paint Windows	12	•					•
Sprouting Carrots	57				•		
Sticky Mural	151						•
Stomp, Stomp, Stomp; Tippy, Tippy, Toe Chant	22	•				•	
Story Bag	28		•				
Story Bell	106		•			•	
Streamer Fun	108					•	•
Street Sweepers	85					•	
Tadpole to Frog	155				•		•
Take One and Pass It On Paper Chain	25	•					•
Talking Tube	21	•	•				
Tap Math	109			•		•	
Teacher, May I?	47		•	•			
Things That Crawl, Creep, and Fly	147				•	•	•
Things We Like to Do	30		•				
Through the Year	133–141					•	•
Tiptoe Chase	76				•	•	
Tissue Paper Berries	32		•	•			•
Towel Fun	92					•	
Transportation	123						•
Truck Math Time	47			•		•	•
Tunneling	160					•	•
Upside-Down Snake Stretches	78				•	•	
Using Our Body Parts	95					•	
Volume Up, Volume Down	111					•	•
Wake Up, Sleepy Bears	97				•	•	

Activity	Page	A	B	C	D	E	F
Walking Tour	68					•	
Weather	148				•	•	•
Weaving Net	153					•	•
What Can You Do?	19	•	•				
What Is the Weather?	56				•		
Whistle	91					•	
Who Lives in a Duplex?	12	•	•				•
Who Lives in a House?	12	•					•
Who Lives in an Apartment?	12	•					•
Whooo Is Calling?	72				•	•	
The Wind Is Moving Air	56			•			
Window Shade City	12	•					•
Winter	122					•	•
Woodland Animals	121					•	•
Yes and No	14	•	•				
Zebra Steps	90			•	•	•	

Social and Emotional Development

Name Game

Materials: large rubber ball

Try this circle activity at the beginning of the school year to help children learn each other's names. Sit with children in a large circle, making sure that everyone has plenty of space. Show children how to sit with their legs open in a *V* shape. Hold a large rubber ball in your hands. Say your name and the name of one of the children and then gently roll the ball to that child. Have that child say his name and the name of another child before rolling the ball to that child. Once a child has caught and rolled the ball, have the child sit cross-legged until everyone has had a turn. Then, play the game again.

To make the game simpler, have each child roll the ball back to you instead of to another child. Once children have mastered the basics of the game, let them roll the ball to each other.

Challenge children to pass the ball to each other as quickly as possible. Use a timer each time they play the game. Talk about playing quickly but carefully so that the ball does not roll out of the circle. Keep a chart with their times written on it. Ask children, "What was your shortest time? What was your longest time?"

Use this game format to learn new things about the children. For example, in addition to having them say their names, have them say how old they are, what their favorite colors are, what they like to eat for breakfast, or some other interesting facts about themselves.

Pass on a Hand Hug

Use this activity at the beginning of any circle time activity, especially if one of the children looks a bit sad. At the beginning of circle time, ask children to join hands with you and each other in a circle. Gently squeeze the hand of one of the children next to you. Tell that child you've just given her a "hand hug." Ask her to pass it on by gently squeezing the hand of the child next to her. Let children continue around the circle until the "hand hug" gets back to you.

Encourage children to start a "hand hug" exchange when they feel the need for a friend.

Simon Says

In advance, prepare a list of directions based on where children live and the names of family members. Word directions to include as many of the children from the group as possible and list something fun they should do. Be certain to include all of the children in several of the directions.

At circle time, have children stand. Explain that when you give a direction, everyone should listen carefully. They should follow the directions only if it relates to them.

Suggested directions and actions

If you have a brother . . .	. . . stand on one leg like a stork.
If you walk to school . . .	. . . march in place.
If anyone in your family is named Joe . . .	. . . raise your right hand.
If you have a pet . . .	. . . bark like a dog.
If anyone in your family has curly hair . . .	. . . wiggle your eyebrows.
If your home is near a grocery store . . .	. . . pretend to eat a banana.
If you live in an apartment . . .	. . . hop twice like a kangaroo.
If anyone in your family likes pizza . . .	. . . roar like a lion.
In anyone in your family wears glasses . . .	. . . walk like a duck.

The Mirror and Me

Materials: hand mirror, preferably plastic for safety; music

Learn about each other with this informative group activity. Have children sit in a circle. Give one child the hand mirror. Begin playing some music and have children carefully pass the mirror around the circle. Stop the music. Then, ask the child who has the mirror a question about herself. Start the music again and continue playing the game, stopping and starting the music as needed until everyone has had a turn.

The next time you do this activity, have the child with the mirror listen while classmates take turns telling one thing they like about her.

Who Lives in a House?

Materials: wooden craft sticks, construction paper

Respecting others is at the heart of this activity. Give each child five wooden craft sticks. Have each child glue the sticks onto a sheet of construction paper in the shape of a house. After the glue is dry, have children color the windows and the door.

Sponge Paint Windows

Materials: construction paper, paint, sponges

This activity will invite conversation about multiple people or families living in one building. Give each child one sheet of construction paper with a large rectangle drawn on it. Tell children that these are big apartment buildings. Provide each child with paint and some sponges cut into small squares. Have children sponge paint windows on the apartment buildings. After the paintings are dry, have children color in trees, people, clouds, etc.

Who Lives in an Apartment?

Materials: white butcher paper, magazines

This activity will help children understand that many people live in an apartment building. Draw the outline of an apartment building on a very large sheet of paper and tape it to the wall or floor. Have children cut out pictures of people from magazines and paste them in the apartment building.

Who Lives in a Duplex?

Materials: white construction paper

Another popular residential option is presented in this activity. Discuss duplexes and townhouses with children. Assign partners and ask children to choose a friend with whom they would like to live in a duplex. Give partners a large sheet of construction paper. Have each child draw one side of a house. Write the names of the two children who are sharing the duplex on top of the paper. Ask partners to take turns telling the rest of the class about their house. Which side belongs to which child? What makes their house special?

Window Shade City

Materials: discarded plastic window shade or plastic tablecloth, permanent markers

The group will create their own community in this activity. First, draw the streets of a city on the window shade. Then, have children take turns drawing in their own houses or apartment buildings. (If using a permanent marker, watch children carefully.) Children will enjoy creating the city where they all live. Have them add stores, gas stations, etc. Keep the window shade city in your classroom. Children will have fun driving cars and trucks on it during play time.

Outdoor Circle Time

Materials: chalk or large sheets of butcher paper or art paper with crayons

Children can openly share their choices in the circle. If it's a nice day, move circle time outside. On a concrete patio or other smooth playground surface, draw a large circle with chalk. If you can't go outside, use crayons and a large sheet of butcher paper or art paper.

Divide the circle you drew into six or eight sections. Label each section with a different option or draw pictures to represent the choices (numbers, pets, fruits, games, etc.).

Read or name the word or the picture in each section of the circle. Have children take turns making one tally mark in the section of the circle that represents their favorite option.

Have children count together to learn which choice was the group's favorite.

Erase and repeat with other choices.

Show Me Your Favorite Color

Materials: a large pile of colored blocks, chips, or game markers (any type of manipulative as long as the items are the same shape and size and come in a large variety of colors representing the children's favorites), large plastic bowl or other container

Show children that individual differences are appropriate and acceptable. Place the colorful manipulatives in a pile in the center of the circle next to the empty container.

Ask each child to take one manipulative in her favorite color from the pile, name the color, and place it in the container.

When everyone has added one manipulative, point out how many different colors are in the container. Tell children that it is because people are different. Not everyone likes the same color.

Yes and No

Materials: red and green construction paper, marker

Expressing your own opinions and respecting others are at the heart of this activity. Before the activity begins, cut red and green construction paper into fourths to make small signs. Use a marker to write *Yes* on all of the green signs and *No* on all of the red signs. Make a green sign and a red sign for each child.

Have children sit in a circle. Discuss opinions with them. Explain that an opinion is the way a person feels about something; it isn't something that is right or wrong. Explain that different people have different opinions. Tell children that we should all respect each other's opinions even when they are not the same as ours.

Now, let children explore their own opinions and discover how they are alike or different from everyone else's. Pass out a green *Yes* sign and a red *No* sign to each child. Have children hold their signs in their laps. Then, ask children a *yes* or *no* question such as the following:

Do you like animals?

Is pink your favorite color?

Is pizza the most delicious food you've ever tasted?

Do you like to go swimming?

Would you like a dog for a pet?

Would you like to fly in an airplane?

Do you like snowy days the best?

At the park, do you like swinging on the swings the most?

Would you like to ride on a train?

Have each child hold up the sign that describes how he feels about the question. Count the green signs and the red signs. Have the children look around. Ask them if all of their friends have the same opinion as they do. Reinforce the idea that people have different opinions about things and that their opinions should be respected.

Friendship Quilt

Materials: one copy of the quilt block below for each student, crayons, paints, or markers

To promote a caring community of learners, invite children to make a friendship quilt. Cut out copies of the quilt block for each child. The quilt will be more interesting if you copy the blocks on different colors of construction paper. Ask each child to draw a picture of herself and a friend doing something together. Remember that a friend might be a four-legged one!

At circle time, help children arrange the drawings to form a quilt pattern. If you have an odd number of students, encourage children to make more than one drawing or do some yourself so that it comes out even. Turn the papers over and tape together from the back with clear tape. Display in your classroom as a Friends' Day decoration.

Happy Hands, Sad Hands

Materials: construction paper cut into hand shapes

Play this game after noticing children fighting, hitting, pushing, or otherwise using their hands in inappropriate ways. Have children stand in a circle. Begin with this rhyme:

> Let's hold hands and circle 'round.
> *(Hold hands in a circle and walk around.)*
>
> Now everyone, please sit down.
> *(Sit down.)*
>
> Place your hands in front of you.
> *(Place hands in lap.)*
>
> And, talk about what they can do.
>
> *Patty Claycomb*

Explain to the children that "happy hands" are hands that do things to make others happy. "Sad hands" are hands that hurt others and make them sad. Have the children think of ways they use their happy hands, such as waving, rocking a baby, holding a friend's hand, or softly patting someone. Then, ask them to think of ways to use sad hands, such as pushing or shoving, throwing toys, grabbing a toy from someone else, or punching or hitting. Ask children which kinds of hands they would rather be around. Have them tell you ways to use happy hands today.

Cut hand shapes out of construction paper. Draw a happy face on half of the hand shapes and a sad face on the other half. Place the hand shapes facedown on the floor. Let each child turn over a hand. If a happy face is showing, have the children name a way to use hands nicely. If a sad face is showing, let the child tell of a way that hands can hurt.

Emotions Die Roll

Materials: Make a copy of the Emotions Die pattern (page 18) and glue it to tagboard. When dry, cut and assemble into a die as directed. The completed project is a tagboard die showing an emotion face on each side.

Children will learn to recognize and identify their feelings. Have children sit in a circle. Show the die and have them name the emotion shown on each side of the die. Allow a variety of answers for each; one child might read a face as angry while another child reads it as frustrated. Tell children that they will each have a turn rolling the die. When a child has rolled the die, have her name the emotion shown on the face of the child. Then, have her name a few things that might make her feel that way. Last, have her describe a time when she felt that emotion. Continue until each child has had a turn to roll the die.

A-A-R-G-H!

Feelings aren't good or bad, they just *are*. Help children learn how to express their feelings appropriately with this activity. Standing on the circle, invite someone to think of a feeling, a sound that expresses that feeling, and an action to go with the feeling. For example, you might start the ball rolling by saying, "When I feel angry, it sounds like this: A-A-R-G-H!, and it looks like this: (Stomp up and down.) Now, you try it." (Everybody goes "a-a-r-g-h" and stomps.) Invite as many children as want to show a feeling. If they get stumped, make some suggestions such as, "What does it sound and look like when you are excited? What does it sound and look like when you are lonely?", etc.

Emotions Die

Directions

Cut out along the thick line.

Fold on the thin lines.

To secure the die, glue the flaps or tape the die together.

What Can You Do?

You could introduce this activity by reading *Mr. Brown Can Moo! Can You?* by
Dr. Seuss to the group at circle time.

Tell children something wonderful (and silly) you can do. Remind children that they
can do many wonderful things too. Go around the circle and ask each child, "What is
something wonderful you can do?" Be enthusiastic and praise each child for whatever
he can do.

Recite this poem to children. Then, talk about how each of us has different talents and
how that's what makes us all great.

Can You?

Can you skip and hop?
Can you spin a top?
Can you bark like a dog?
Can you croak like a frog?
Can you roller skate?
Can you bake a cake?
Can you button your shirt?
Can you zip your skirt?
Can you climb a tree?
Can you buzz like a bee?
Can you spin around?
Can you giggle like a clown?
Can you write your name?
Can you play a game?
Can you make a wish?
Can you wash a dish?
Can you hammer a nail?
Can you juggle a pail?
Can you dance a jig?
Can you catch a pig?

Can you ride a bike?
Can you go for a hike?
Can you swim in a pool
Like the little fishes do?
Can you dance in the rain?
Can you drive a train?
Can you wiggle your nose?
Can you touch your toes?
Can you hop like a bunny
Or tell a joke that's funny?
Can you count to ten?
And back again?
Can you read a book?
Can you bait a hook?
Can you paint a house?
Can you squeak like a mouse?
If I sing a song,
Can you sing along?
Can you tie your shoe?
What else can you do?

Encourage children to add more couplets using this format.

Imagination Nature Walk

When it's too awful to go outside, and everyone is feeling antsy, try this. At circle time, ask children to lie on their backs. Turn the lights down low and read the following story, pausing where indicated.

Imagination Nature Walk

Is everyone comfortable? Good. Now, we're going to go for a walk in our imaginations. But first, we want to relax and quiet our bodies. First, relax your toes. Good. Now, relax your legs and knees; relax your tummy; relax your back; relax your hands; relax your arms; relax your neck; relax your face. Good. Now, imagine that you are standing in front of a door. You open the door and see that it is a warm, sunny day. You step out the door and see a path going into some woods. You follow the path, and as you go into the trees, you see a lot of sweet-smelling flowers blooming in the woods. Lean down and smell one of the flowers. Now, you hear birds singing. You look up. A beautiful bird is in the tree above you. Listen to his song. You start to walk again. You hear someone calling your name. You see a friend coming toward you. You are very happy to see your friend, and your friend is happy to see you. You go farther into the woods together. You see a big patch of ripe berries. Pick some and put them in a bucket. Many butterflies are in the air, and the air is warm. You are happy! You and your friend talk and laugh and play.

It's getting late. It's time to go home. You and your friend walk to the edge of the woods together and say good-bye. You walk back on the path to the door you came out of. You go in the door. You are back in the circle. When you are ready, open your eyes.

Go around the circle and have children tell about their imaginary nature walk.

Talking Tube

Materials: long cardboard tube

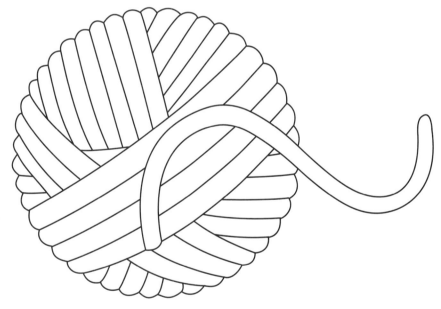

Waiting for a turn to speak is a challenge for young children,
but a talking tube can make this task a little easier for them.
Decorate a long cardboard tube with crayons to make a
"talking tube" and show it to the children. Explain that this tube is similar to the Native
American talking stick. Many Native American tribes use a talking stick whenever a group
of people gathers together. Only the person holding the stick can talk. Everyone else has
to listen. Then, the person holding the stick hands it to the next person to talk.

Sit with children in a circle. Hold the talking tube and say your name. Pass the tube to the
child beside you and have that child say his name. Continue until each child has said
his name. Then, ask children to think of their favorite things to do. Pass the talking tube to
one of the children and have him name a favorite activity. Have the other children who
have not had a turn silently raise their hands. Let the child with the talking tube give it
to a child who has a hand raised. Repeat until each child has had a turn. After children
have practiced with the talking tube, you may wish to use it when you want to have a
group discussion in which one person at a time may talk.

The Circle of Noise

Materials: yarn

Help children learn to
distinguish between inside
noise and outside noise
with this activity. Cut a
15-foot (4.6-m) length of
yarn and arrange it on
the floor in a circle. Have
children stand around the
circle of yarn to make the
"circle of noise." Explain
to them that you will make
quiet and loud noises.
When you make a quiet
noise, such as dropping a
paper clip to the ground
or tapping drinking straws
together, have them stand
inside the circle of noise. When you make a loud sound, such as beating a drum or
banging blocks together, have them stand outside the circle of noise. Remind them to
make quiet noises when they are indoors and to save their loud noises for outside.

Lizards Inside, Dinosaurs Outside

To illustrate the difference between "indoor" and "outdoor" voices, do this activity. Ask children to stand up just outside the circle line. Explain that this is "dinosaur land." This is like being outdoors where it is OK to roar as loud as a dinosaur. Encourage everyone to roar and stomp around a bit. Now, invite children to step inside the circle. This is "lizard land." Lizards are very quiet. Encourage everyone to tiptoe and talk softly. Invite children to step back and forth across the circle and practice their dinosaur and lizard voices. Remind them to be lizards inside and dinosaurs outside.

Stomp, Stomp, Stomp; Tippy, Tippy, Toe Chant

Practice indoor and outdoor noise levels with this chant. March around the circle as you chant it.

> Stomp, stomp, stomp,
> Tippy, tippy, toe,
> 'Round and 'round the circle we go.
>
> Outdoors we make
> LOTS OF NOISE.
> Indoors we're
> Quiet girls and boys.

Quiet Countdown

To get the volume turned down, begin circle time with a quiet countdown. Say, "ten" very loud. Then, get softer and softer as you count down, until "one" is so quiet that you can hardly hear it. Invite children to count down with you several times to practice counting, as well as to practice quieting down.

After children are familiar with quiet countdown, recite the alphabet, starting loud and getting quieter as you go.

Beanbag Games

These beanbag activities help with coordination, fine and large motor skills, cognitive development, and social skills.

Beanbag Circle Walk
Have each child put a beanbag on her head and walk around the circle. Once everyone can get around the circle without the beanbag falling off, try some new things such as walking backward, skipping, and crawling. Invite children to think of some other ways to move.

Pass the Beanbag
Put all of the beanbags in a basket or a bucket. Have each child choose a beanbag and pass the basket on. Use a stopwatch and challenge students to see how quickly they can empty the basket.

Beanbag Relay Race
Use two beanbags for this activity. Start one beanbag around the circle in one direction and the other beanbag around the circle in the other direction. See which beanbag makes it back to you first. Invite different children to start the race. Do this several times and compare. Ask children, "Which direction wins most often? Why do you think that happens?"

For other versions of the relay, have children pass the beanbags behind their backs or with their eyes closed.

After the children have mastered the concept of beanbag relays, have each child put the beanbag on his head, then nod and tip it into the next child's lap.

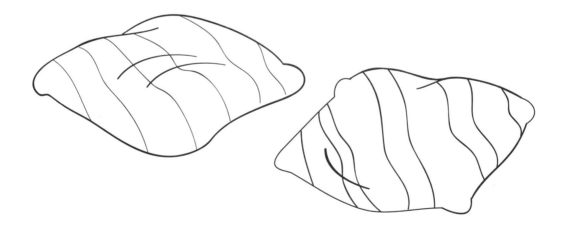

Kick the Beanbag
Have children stand on a starting line a few at a time. Place a beanbag about 2 feet (0.6 m) in front of each child. Have children try to kick the beanbag forward without losing their balance. Then, have them repeat with the other foot. Have them try again with the beanbag about 3 feet (0.9 m) away. (This activity is also fun to do outside in the snow. Kicking in the snow and with boots on is a challenge!)

Beanbag "It"
Have children form a single circle, facing the center with their hands behind their backs. One child is "it" and stands outside the circle. This child walks around the circle and drops the beanbag into another child's hands. The child who was given the beanbag chases "it" and tries to tag him or her before "it" can reach the empty place in the circle. If the child tags "it," he or she gets the beanbag and is the new "it."

Fall Color Beanbag Toss
Gather four shoe boxes and cover them with red, brown, yellow, and orange construction or contact paper. Make beanbags from coordinating material and beans. Have children take turns picking up a beanbag, naming its color, and trying to toss it into the matching box.

Beanbag Fun
Have children walk in a single circle while throwing beanbags into the air and catching them. Tell them that, on your signal, they will drop the beanbags. Then, they will jump, hop, or leap over the scattered beanbags. On your signal again, they will each pick up the nearest beanbag and begin playing catch with themselves again.

Sharing Fair

Plan a "sharing fair" with activities that illustrate and practice good reasons for sharing. Do some or all of the following:

Ask children to bring snacks to share. For example, a third of the class could bring crackers, a third could bring cheese, and a third could bring apple juice. At snack time, have everyone help assemble the snack and share it.

Have children bring one special toy each that they are willing to share. At circle time, have a show-and-tell. During free play, encourage toy sharing.

Collect cans of food or clothing to share with a local soup kitchen or homeless shelter.

Invite grandparents or other elders to share memories and stories with the children.

 **(See page 2.)**

Take One and Pass It On Paper Chain

Have strips of colorful paper, a marker, and a glue stick at the circle. Start a discussion about sharing by asking children what sorts of things they enjoy sharing with friends or family members. Pass the paper strips around, instructing each child to "take one and pass the rest on." When everyone has a strip, go around the circle and write what each child said he enjoyed sharing on his strip. Pass the glue stick around and help children make a paper chain. Hang it on the wall or drape it on a plant.

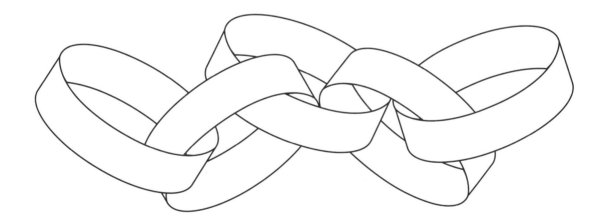

If You Were a Carpenter

This activity encourages children to learn about and create actions for various occupations.

Read each of the couplets. Have children make up actions for each verse.

If You Were a Carpenter

If you were a carpenter, you could build a house
For a dog, or a cat, or a person, or a mouse.
If you were a mechanic, you could fix a car.
You'd check the tires so we could drive far.
If you were a doctor, you'd make people well.
Instead of being sick, they'd soon feel swell.
If you were a baker, you'd make lots of bread
For Aaron, Anna, Anthony, and Uncle Fred.
If you were a plumber, you could fix the tub
For my rubber ducky—rub-a-dub-dub.
If you were a farmer, you could grow corn and peas,
Pumpkins for autumn, or maybe pretty trees.
If you were a pilot, you could fly an airplane
And take many people to Timbuktu or Spain.
If you were an astronaut, you would go up in space.
Look down upon the earth—what a beautiful place!

For more circle time activities on community helpers, see pages 155–160.

Cinderella Shoe Match

Materials: large brown paper bag

Ask each child to take off one shoe and put it in the bag. (You too.) Mix up the shoes. Let children take turns taking one shoe from the bag and matching it to its owner. The owner of the shoe can take the next turn.

Greetings from Around the World

At circle time, teach children to say "hello" in several languages. Here are a few to get you started:

Chinese:	*Nee-ho*	Czech:	*A-hoy*
French:	*Bonjour*	German:	*Gooten taag*
Greek:	*Yah-soo*	Hebrew:	*Shalom*
Hawaiian:	*A-low-ha*	Italian:	*Chow*
Norwegian:	*Hallo*	Polish:	*Witag*
Spanish:	*Oh-la*	Swahili:	*Jambo*
Swedish:	*Hey*	Turkish:	*Merhaba selam*

English Language Learners can ask their parents and grandparents to teach them to say "hello" their languages and share what they learned with the class at circle time the next day.

Use online translation Web sites to find other common words such as *please, thank you,* or *you're welcome* in several languages to share with children.

Cognitive Development

Story Bag

Materials: objects for storytelling, cloth or paper bag, ball of yarn

Teach children the art of storytelling without a book. Collect a variety of interesting, nonbreakable items to use while telling a story. For example, you could collect a toy car, a plastic animal, a small stuffed animal, a spoon, a block, a game piece, a small book, a crayon, a pair of sunglasses, and a hat. Place all of the objects in a cloth or paper bag.

To play the story bag game, start a simple story with an opening line such as "One day as I was walking down the street . . . ." Pause and ask the child sitting next to you to take one of the objects out of the bag. Incorporate the object into your story. If the child takes a spoon out of the bag, you could continue your story like this: ". . . I was eating a bowl of chocolate pudding. All of a sudden . . . ." Ask another child to pull a new object from the story bag. Incorporate that object into your story as you continue. Keep telling your story until all of the objects are used. As the children become familiar with this activity, let them help you tell the story. Eventually, the children will be able to make up a story all by themselves.

Older children may also enjoy this storytelling variation. Have children sit in a circle. Tell them that they will make a story web. Let them help you choose a topic for the story, such as a day in the park, a day at the beach, or playing with friends. With a ball of yarn in one hand, start telling your story. When you arrive at a stopping point, hold onto the end of the yarn and roll the rest of it to one of the children. Have that child continue the story for a while, hold onto the yarn, and then roll the ball to another child. (Let the children who do not wish to play say "pass" and roll the ball of yarn to another child in the circle.) When the story is finished, have the children look at the story "web" they have made on the floor.

Record the story bag stories as you and the children tell them and let the children illustrate them.

Make Stories Live

Materials: picture books with large, colorful illustrations

Reading to children and telling stories are probably the best things that a teacher or parent can do to increase language development. The more children are exposed to language, the more language they will use and understand. Announce to the children that today's story will have no written words on the page. The story will be created using the illustrations to inspire everyone's creativity. Showing the pictures on the first page, ask children, "Who are the characters in the story? Are they large or small? Do they live in the city, in the country, or in a jungle? Are these photographs or drawn illustrations?" Then, go through the pages of the book, encouraging children to keep the story moving forward by reminding them what has happened on previous pages. The children will learn to add details to the story as they watch your expression and share in the enthusiasm of the group. Preschoolers enjoy repetition, so "read" through the story a second time and have children reenact parts of the story or retell it.

My Bandage Story

Materials: variety of small adhesive bandages

Boo-boos are always of interest to preschoolers, so this can really be a fun activity. Give each child one bandage. Tell children to put the bandages anywhere they want to on their bodies—head, hand, knee, foot, etc. Then, ask each child to make up a story about how he or she got hurt. Some children will retell real experiences, and other children will make up exciting "pretend" stories.

Concept Circle Game

Listening and following directions are skills that can be taught using large motor skills in this indoor or outdoor activity.

Have children sit in a large circle. Begin the game with simple prepositions such as *up* and *down*. Say to the children, "Everyone stand up. Everyone sit down." Have the children say the words with you. Repeat this sequence three to four times.

Continue with more concepts such as opposites: "Point to the inside of the circle. Now, point to the outside of the circle." Repeat. "Whisper your name. (quiet). Now, shout your name (loud)." Repeat. "Point to a boy. Now, point to a girl." Continue adding more concepts to the game. Children will enjoy the repetition and movement along with the language development.

My House

Materials: dollhouse and dolls or flannel board and felt people

Communicating about family builds self-confidence and enriches language development. Begin a discussion of "who lives at my house." Let each child have a turn placing all of his or her family members in the house or on the flannel board. Encourage each child to name all of the people and tell you something about each of them.

When preparing the dolls or the flannel board people, be sure to include grandparent figures and figures that represent pets. You can also encourage conversation about who is the biggest, littlest, oldest, youngest, etc.

I'm Thinking

This guessing game encourages the use of logic and problem solving. While in a circle, begin describing a child in the class. Say, "I'm thinking about a boy." Keep adding details and encourage children to listen to the clues before guessing. "This boy is wearing a blue shirt. This boy has brown eyes. This boy likes cheese sandwiches." As children learn this skill, have them describe someone in the class, the school, or the community that will be familiar to everyone.

Things We Like to Do

Materials: chart paper, magazines

Children enjoy reading about themselves in a variety of classroom displays. Make a chart titled "Things We Like to Do." List the children's names on the chart. Next, have children cut out pictures from magazines of things they like to do (toys, games, activities, etc.) and paste them under their names on the chart. Some children may enjoy drawing pictures of things they like.

When the chart is complete, let each child tell about her picture and interests.

Letter Basket

Materials: basket, small objects that begin with sounds children have learned (ball for the letter *b*, small stuffed cat for the letter *c*, etc.), CD player, fast-paced music

This activity reinforces letter recognition though music. Before starting the music, review the objects in the basket to be sure that all of the children are familiar with the names of each. For example, they will want to know whether to say "cat" or "kitten." Start the music and pass the basket around the circle. When you stop the music, have the child holding the basket take out one object and tell everyone what letter its name starts with. Start the music again and continue the activity until everyone has had a turn. You may either have the children keep the objects during the game or return them to the basket to be chosen again. Base this choice on the mastery level of the children participating.

Fly or Run?

Materials: pictures of flying and running animals that begin with sounds children have learned

This large motor activity reviews letter sounds. In the circle, hold up a picture of an animal. Have children say the animal name and the letter it starts with. Then, tell them to jump up and either flap their arms or run in place based on the type of animal. For example, for a picture of a tiger, the children would say, "*Tiger* starts with *t*" and then jump up and run in place. For a picture of a butterfly, the children would say, "*Butterfly* starts with *b*" and then jump up and flap their arms.

Fabric Lotto

Materials: 9" x 9" (22.8 cm x 22.8 cm) squares of poster board, pinking shears, 2" x 2" (5 cm x 5 cm) assorted fabric squares

This activity gives children the experience of observing and matching printed pieces of fabric. Cut several squares of poster board. Then, cut two squares of each fabric, using pinking shears so that the fabric will not ravel. Glue one of each of the two alike squares to the poster board. Then, place nine different squares on each board. Each board should be different. The second square of each fabric will remain as a swatch for you or the child who leads the activity.

To play the game, give a board to each child. Hold up one fabric swatch at a time. If a child has fabric on his board exactly like the one you are holding, he should take the swatch and place it on top of the matching fabric. Continue the game until everyone has matched all of the fabric on their boards.

You can make this game simpler or more complex by varying the fabrics used. For example, construct boards with solid fabrics only, plaid fabrics only, or striped fabrics only.

Tissue Paper Berries

Materials: craft tissue paper, construction paper

In this activity, children develop pre-writing skills by identifying specific letters.

Cut tissue paper into 2-inch (5-cm) squares. (Cutting rows and layers of tissue paper will speed up the process.)

Cut 10 to 12 sheets of construction paper in half. Decide what letters you want the children to recognize and print one letter on each sheet of construction paper.

Place the tissue paper, construction paper letters, and glue at the children's work area.

Have children take tissue paper squares and roll them with their fingers into "berries" (round balls). Let the children make more berries and place them next to their letters.

Next, have children squeeze glue onto the letter outline and place their berries onto the glue.

Questions, Questions

Materials: counters (any colorful math manipulatives)

Children strengthen their listening skills as they play this game.

Divide children into two teams. Let them pick team names. (You might give them a choice of two or three names.) Tell children that they will play a question-and-answer game. Explain that they must first listen carefully to the question and then let the team whose turn it is answer the question to earn one point. If the first team is unable to answer the question, the other team gets a chance. Each time a team gets a point, place a counter on that team's side. During the game, have children count aloud together the number of points each team has. The children should be able to tell you which team has the most points. At the end of the game, announce that each team has won. Make up fun rewards such as a trip outside, a free recess, etc.

Example: Team names—Butterflies vs. Caterpillars

Question to Butterflies: "What has leaves and a trunk and grows in the ground?"

If the Butterflies answer correctly, they get one point. Then, it is the Caterpillars' turn. If the Butterflies answer incorrectly, the Caterpillars get a chance to answer the question.

I Am a Tree

Materials: *The Giving Tree* by Shel Silverstein or *The Elephant Tree* by Penny Dale

Children use their bodies to learn about trees in this activity.

Read children one of the stories about trees. Discuss how trees have roots, buds, leaves, and trunks. Go outside and have children touch the different trees around the school. Let them look at the branches and the roots. Encourage the children to describe the textures of the trees. Tell the children that they are going to grow like trees. Have them plant their feet firmly on the ground, bend down, and become tiny trees. Tell them that their bodies are the trunks, their arms are the branches, and their fingers are the leaves.

Have children slowly grow toward the sun by moving their bodies up and spreading their arms and fingers toward the sun. Next, tell the children to sway in the wind and move their bodies, keeping their feet in one place. Remind children that roots keep trees firmly planted in the ground.

How Many Ways?

Children expand their problem-solving skills as they participate in this activity. Ask children one of the following questions. Encourage them to think of as many responses as they can. Support children's creative thinking by accepting all of their answers as correct, even the "silly" ones. Continue with as many questions as you and the children would like.

How many ways can you get across the room?
How many ways can you say "hello"?
How many ways can you go down the stairs?
How many ways can you eat peanut butter?
How many ways can you show you are happy?
How many ways can you get across a river?
How many ways can you play with a ball?

Rhyming Riddles

Encourage children's language and listening skills with this activity. Read one of the following rhyming riddles to children. Have them tell you what the riddle is about. Remind them that the name of the item rhymes with the word given in the riddle.

I am thinking of something that is straight or curly and rhymes with chair. What is it? (hair)

I am thinking of something that is red, white, and blue and rhymes with tag. What is it? (flag)

I am thinking of something that has windows and doors and rhymes with mouse. What is it? (house)

Once the children are familiar with this game, let them think of their own riddles to say and solve.

Let's Talk about Honesty

Materials: *Jamaica's Find* by Juanita Havill (Sandpiper, 1987), a stuffed animal (a dog like Edgar dog would be great)

Young children learn right and wrong from parents and teachers, as well as from each other. They watch movies and read books. They see examples in the behavior of others. This book provides an excellent opportunity to discuss honesty with children.

As you read *Jamaica's Find* with children at circle time, give them time to observe the delightful watercolor illustrations on each page. Talk about the pictures with the children.

After reading the book, ask questions to help children explore the concept of honesty.

Why do you think Jamaica turned in the hat she found?

Why do you think Jamaica didn't turn in the stuffed dog she found at the park?

Jamaica's mother said, "Maybe the dog doesn't fit you either?" What do you think she meant?

Why do you think keeping the stuffed dog didn't make Jamaica happy?

Do you think the stuffed dog Jamaica found was worth a lot of money?

Who thought the stuffed dog was very valuable?

How would you feel if you were Kristin and lost Edgar dog?

Why do you think Jamaica felt good when she helped Kristin find Edgar dog?

Hand the stuffed animal to the child who volunteers to answer and let her use Edgar dog to do the "talking." Have children pass the stuffed animal around the circle to indicate the next speaker.

Ask:

If Edgar dog could talk, what would he say to Jamaica when she found him and took him home?

If Edgar dog could talk, what would he say to Kristin when she found him?

If Edgar dog could talk, what advice do you think he would give the children?

I Am Not Afraid of Monsters

Children have many fears. They may be afraid of the dark, imaginary monsters, dogs, spiders, thunderstorms, or being in unfamiliar situations. Remember to respect children's feelings; their fears are very real to them. Do not allow other children to make fun of a classmate's fear.

Not all fears are bad, however. Some types of fears are healthy and can keep children out of trouble. Children's fears are often based on the unknown. You can help children overcome their fears by giving them confidence.

Materials: *Go Away, Big Green Monster!* by Ed Emberley (Little, Brown and Company, 1992), sidewalk chalk

Read *Go Away, Big Green Monster!* to the children.

Follow up by holding circle time outside on the playground or on a sidewalk near the school. Draw a big scary monster with chalk.

Have children join hands in a circle around the drawing. Using your bravest voice, say, "I'm not afraid of this big old monster. Look what I can do."

Stomp the monster and wipe out part of the drawing with your shoe. Ask for volunteers by saying, "Who else isn't afraid of this monster? Show me what you can do to this monster."

Let children take turns stomping on the monster and erasing parts of it. Ask children to think of some creative ways to "erase" the monster (use water, rub with a paper towel, sweep with a broom).

Use this opportunity to talk about the difference between "real" and "pretend" by asking a series of questions such as the following. Encourage children to respond as a group.

Are talking dragons real?	Are bananas real?
Are cars real?	Can cows fly?
Can elephants talk to people?	Can penguins drive cars?
Can trees walk around?	Can dinosaurs stomp on you?
Can spiders spin webs?	Can mosquitoes bite you?
Can (name a familiar cartoon character) visit your house?	
Can a scary character on TV get out of the TV?	

Changes

Materials: *Sky Tree* by Thomas Locker (HarperCollins, 2001)

Read *Sky Tree* to the children. As you read this lyrical text, encourage children to observe the details of the beautiful illustrations in this glorious celebration of nature and change throughout the seasons. As the tree changes, so does the sky, the ground below the tree, the river, and the mountains in the background.

When you finish reading, ask questions to encourage a discussion about changes.

• How did the tree change?

• Even though the tree changed, was it still the same tree?

• What other changes happen in our lives? (Day turns to night, seasons change, etc.)

• Do people change? How? (Children grow up; what they like to do, eat, or read changes; etc.)

• Do families always stay the same? Why not?

• When a baby is born, is the baby a member of the family?

• If a grandparent or other relative comes to live with you, is that person part of your family?

• If a big brother or sister (or parent) moves to different house, are they still part of your family?

• If a family member moves far away, is that person still part of your family?

• What other kinds of changes can happen in a family?

Are You My Mother?

Materials: *Are You My Mother?* by P. D. Eastman (Random House, 1966), copy of the Mother and Baby Animal Cards (page 39)

Read *Are You My Mother?* to the children. Talk about the different animal mothers and babies shown in the book.

Talk about the book by asking questions such as these:

Why did the mother bird leave her baby?

How did the baby bird feel when he couldn't find his mother?

Did the mother bird come back for her baby as soon as she could?

Help children differentiate between "real" and "pretend" with questions such as these:

Do real animals have mothers?

Do machines such as cars and airplanes have mothers?

Enlarge and copy the animal cards on light cardboard or laminate the page before cutting out the mother and baby cards.

Give each child a baby animal card. Keep the mother animal cards facedown in a pile.

Turn over the mother animal cards one at a time. Ask a child to name the animal. Then ask, "Who has a baby to go with this mother?"

Place your card and the matching baby animal card faceup in the center of the circle.

Let children use the cards for a memory game, matching mothers and baby animals.

Mother and Baby Animal Cards

horse	colt	goose	gosling
duck	duckling	cat	kitten
dog	puppy	rabbit	bunny
hen	chick	pig	piglet
cow	calf	kangaroo	joey
sheep	lamb	bear	cub

How Many?

Materials: five teddy bears, five hats to fit teddy bears, five toys, five books

Strengthen counting and one-to-one correspondence skills with this activity. Set out five teddy bears. Collect five hats, five small toys, and five books. Have the children sit around the teddy bears. Count the teddy bears together. Now, set out three hats. Have one of the children place a hat on each bear. Ask the children if there are enough hats for each bear to have one. How many more do they need? Help the child count the remaining two bears without hats. Then, give him two more hats to place on the teddy bears. Repeat with the toys and the books, starting with a different number of items each time. When all of the teddy bears have their own hats, toys, and books, sing the following song with the children:

> *Sing to the tune of: "Three Blind Mice"*
>
> Five teddy bears,
> Five teddy bears.
> One, two, three, four, five,
> One two, three, four, five.
> Each teddy bear has a hat that's new.
> Each teddy bear has a book to read, too.
> Five teddy bears.
>
> *Gayle Bittinger*

For a fine motor activity, give each child a sheet of construction paper and five precut teddy bear shapes (available from school supply stores). Have children glue their teddy bear shapes onto their papers. Then, give each child five star stickers, five heart stickers, and five circle stickers to add to their teddy bears. Encourage children to count as they glue their bear shapes and add the stars, the hearts, and the circles.

Counting Catches

Materials: ball of yarn (purchased or made with colorful yarn)

This activity helps children practice their counting and eye-hand coordination. Have children stand in a big circle, leaving at least 3 feet (0.9 m) of space between each child. Give one child a ball of yarn. Have her toss it to the next child in the circle. Have that child, in turn, toss the yarn to the next child. As the yarn travels around the circle, have children count each time it is caught. Ask them to tell you how many times the ball of yarn was caught as it went around the circle. Challenge children to see how many times they can catch and count the ball of yarn without dropping it.

Number Match Game

Materials: index cards, construction paper, markers

Make sets of cards numbered 1 to 10 for children and for yourself. Give each child a set. To play the game, hold up a number card from your set. Have children look through their cards to find the one with the matching number and place it on the floor in front of them. Repeat for each number in the set. If you wish, let the children take turns holding up a number card for the others to match.

For younger children, make sets of cards numbered 1 to 5. Write each number in a different color. For older children, make sets of cards numbered 1 to 20 or just cards from 11 to 20.

Turn this into a more active counting experience by numbering 10 sheets of construction paper from 1 to 10. Place the numbered sheets all around the room. Give each child a set of number cards. Have children walk around the room, finding the numbered sheets and placing their matching numbered cards on top of them.

The Ins and Outs of Circles

Materials: large toy hoops or yarn

Children learn positional words using their body parts. Arrange large toy hoops or yarn circles on the floor and have children stand around them. Give directions such as these: "Put your body in the circle. Put one arm out of the circle. Put one leg and one arm in the circle. Put just your head in the circle. Put your head and one more body part in the circle. Let just one body part touch the ground outside the circle." Encourage children to find their own unique ways of following the directions. Some may stand while others sit on the floor or lie on their tummies.

Over and Under the Bridge

Materials: *The Three Billy Goats Gruff* by Janet Stevens (Sandpiper, 2008). This modern version has beautiful illustrations and simple text.

Use children's literature to learn "over" and "under." Read the book or tell the story of The Three Billy Goats Gruff. Discuss the story and ask the children, "Who went over the bridge? Who was under the bridge? What else was over the bridge (sky, air, sunshine)? What else was under the bridge (water, fish, air)?" Now, ask them to think of other things that are over or under something else. Let them share their answers.

One, Two, Pick Up Sticks

Materials: wooden craft sticks, construction paper, markers

Children will learn to recognize numerals and to count. Cut construction paper into fourths. Write the numerals you will be working with (for example, 0–3 or 0–5) on the fourths. Be sure that each fourth has only one numeral written on it, and be sure that each child has a set of four cards.

Give children enough wooden craft sticks to total the numbers they are using. For example, if you are working with the numbers 0–5, each child will need 15 craft sticks. Let children identify each numeral, count out the matching number of wooden craft sticks, and place them on that number. Let them continue this process until all of their cards are complete.

While children are engaged in this activity, assist and observe their math progress. If children are not counting out the number of wooden craft sticks correctly, help them. If they have completed the task incorrectly, they may not be ready for this type of math.

Counting Song

Materials: construction paper or index cards, markers

Number 10 sheets of construction paper or index cards from 1 to 10. Distribute the paper or cards to 10 children. Sing the following counting song with children. As each number is named, have the child holding that number raise it above his head. At the end of the song, give the number cards to different children and sing the song again.

Sing to the tune of: "The Farmer in the Dell"

One, two, three, four, five,
Six, seven, eight, nine, ten.
We can all count from one to ten.
Let's all count again.

Gayle Bittinger

A Box of Circles

Materials: assortment of items, some circle-shaped (jar lids, bottle caps, o-shaped cereal, paper circles), some not circle-shaped

Place the materials in a round hatbox or cookie tin and show the container at circle time. Remove the top from the box and show children that it is a circle, and its outside is round. Now, dump out the contents and spread them on the floor. Tell children that only circles belong in the box. In turn, let them each choose one item and place it in the box. Have all of the children name the chosen item and tell if they agree whether it belongs in the box.

Sorting Circles

Materials: felt, large toy hoop, glue, magnetic strips

From a single color of felt, cut a variety of shapes for the flannel board or glue magnetic strips to the back to use on a whiteboard. Make these in several sizes and include quite a few circles. Place the shapes at random on the flannel board or the whiteboard. Lay a large toy hoop on the floor in front of you and place a large sheet of paper beside it. Explain to children that all of the circles belong in the hoop, and all of the shapes that are not circles belong on the paper. Send several children at a time to the flannel board or whiteboard to select a shape and place it where it belongs.

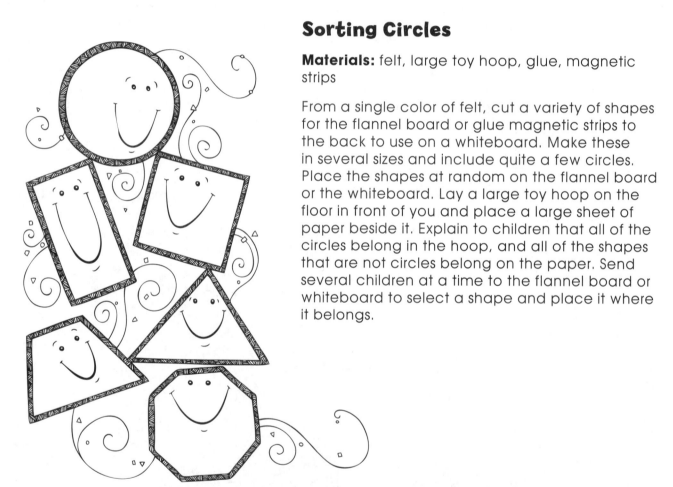

Chocolate Chip Cookie Count

Materials: 2 or 3 different kinds of chocolate chip cookies, copies of the chip and the large cookie patterns (below), one copy of the cookie patterns (page 46) per child, one set of number cards per child with numerals 0–10

Children count and identify numerals in this activity. Discuss the real chocolate chip cookies with children. Ask them how many chips they think are in each cookie. Then, place the enlarged cookie pattern on a table. Give each child a chip pattern and let him or her place it on the large cookie. As children place the chips on the cookie, count them together. If you like, make two large cookie patterns and let children place chips on both cookies (to compare more/less).

Next, give each child a set of the cookies from page 46. (Cut out the cookies so that the children can randomly set them out.) Have children find the cookie with one chip and hold it up or point to it. Continue this process while calling out different numbers. Give each child a set of number cards and have him place the matching numeral on the cookie with that amount of chips. For children that are not at this level yet, give them chip patterns to practice one-to-one correspondence (placing chips on the cookie chips).

At the conclusion of this activity, eat chocolate chip cookies!

Safety First! (See page 2.)

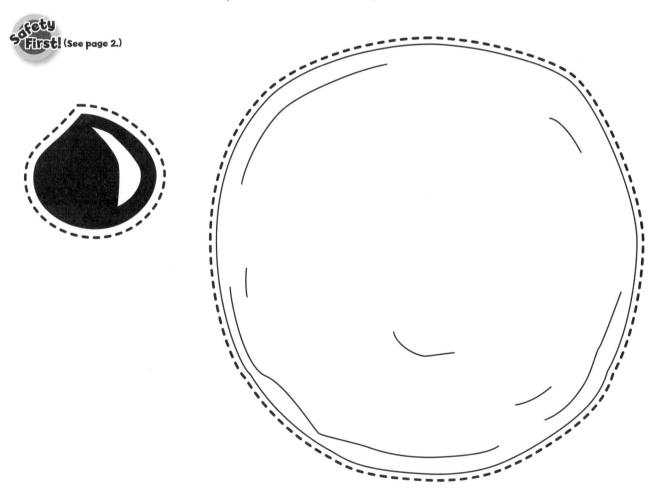

Chocolate Chip Cookie Patterns

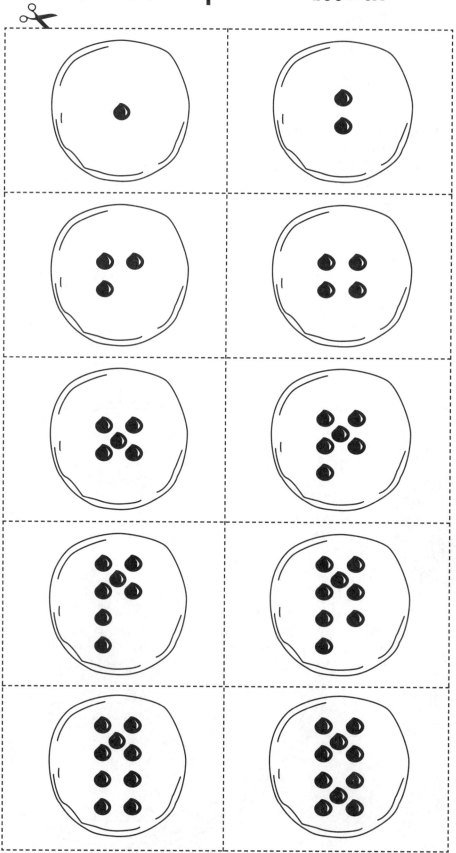

Truck Math Time

Materials: 24" x 36" white sheets of poster board, markers, very small toy trucks, sunflower seeds

Children share toys as they work together on this counting activity. Make "farm boards" with the sheets of poster board. Draw farms with roads and a variety of numbered barns, animal feeders, and trees. Make enough farm boards so that each pair of children has one. Provide children with toy trucks and sunflower seeds to place in the back of their trucks. Have children drive on the roads and deliver sunflower seeds to all of the numbered areas. They should deliver the same amount of seeds as written on each object.

Teacher, May I?

Materials: yarn, string, or masking tape

Children follow directions and count steps in this large motor activity. Set up a starting line and finish line made of yarn, string, or tape. Have a small group of children line up with their toes on the line or the string. Remind them to listen to what you are about to say and practice with them so they understand the game. Tell children that you are going to ask them to take a certain number of steps toward the finish line. Point to the finish line (another line of yarn or string). Then, describe the steps they will take, such as large steps and small steps. Show them what you consider to be a large step and a small step. Once children understand the length of the steps, explain to them that when they cross the finish line, they must sit down and wait for the other children to finish. Have children move the number of steps you desire in specific lengths. Encourage children to count aloud. (Example: "Everyone take three small steps. 1, 2, 3! Now, everyone take one big step and two small steps.")

Fabric Matching

Materials: a variety of fabric samples cut into 4" (10 cm) squares

Divide the fabric squares so that each child receives two or three of each print of the fabric you have selected. Give each child about 15 pieces of fabric.

Show children how to match the fabric squares that are the same by looking at the colors and designs on each square. Let children describe the colors and textures of the fabric pieces.

You can also make matching cards from index cards or squares of construction paper. Draw simple patterns on each card for the children to match. Use the pattern ideas below or cut apart old gift wrap or wallpaper samples.

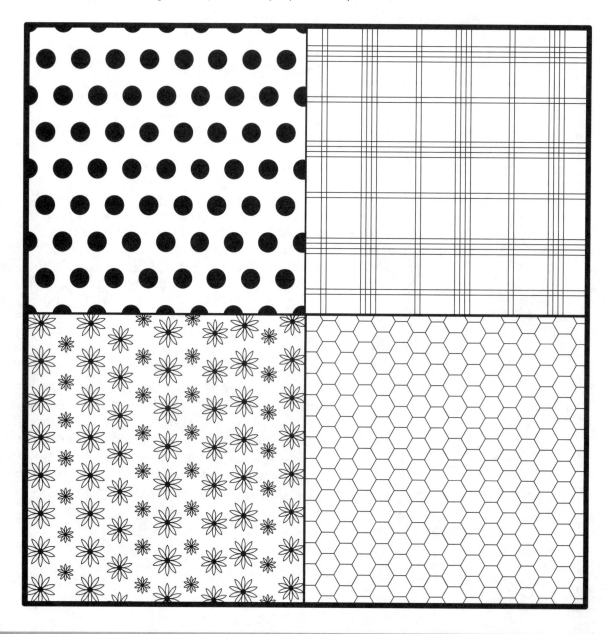

Seashell Sorting

Materials: seashells of various shapes, sizes, and textures

Classify objects in this fun summer activity. Place the seashells out for children to observe and describe. Have children group the shells according to size. Then, have them sequence different-sized shells from smallest to largest. Next, let children group them according to similar shapes.

Encourage children to describe the textures and the colors of the seashells. Ask children different questions about the seashells, such as "Where do seashells come from? Which shell is the biggest? Which shell is the smallest? How many little seashells can you hold in your hand?"

Block Bonanza

Materials: three sizes of unit blocks, construction paper, markers

This fine motor activity integrates math, language, and cutting skills. Discuss the size and the shape of the three sizes of unit blocks. Encourage children to place them in order according to size (small, medium, large).

Give each child three blocks of different sizes. Let children trace the blocks onto construction paper. Next, have children cut out the block shapes.

Have children glue the cut shapes in order from smallest to largest onto a sheet of construction paper. Encourage children to tell you which of the shapes is small, medium, and large.

Birdseed Math

Materials: large bag of birdseed; variety of plastic containers, funnels, spoons; 4 large plastic containers that will hold a large quantity of birdseed; measuring cups

Children pour and practice measurement in this activity. Pour enough birdseed into plastic containers to completely cover the bottom. Place measuring cups, funnels, and spoons in each container of birdseed. Show children how they can use the objects to pour birdseed into the empty containers.

Next, ask the children some questions similar to the following:

1. How does the birdseed feel?

2. What are the different colors and shapes of the seeds?

3. Which container is easiest to pour the birdseed into without spilling any?

4. Which container holds the most birdseed?

5. How many measuring cups does it take to fill up the container?

Place the containers of birdseed in a science or math center. Children love the sensory feeling of birdseed play.

Footprints Frenzy

Materials: construction paper, pencils or crayons, scissors

Tracing and counting footprints reinforces sequencing skills and ordinal numbers. Have children sit in a circle and count the number of shoes they have on their feet. Let children trace an outline of their pair of shoes on five sheets of construction paper using pencils or crayons. Next, have children cut out all 10 of their outlines. Each child should have five pairs of shoe outlines.

Help children write the numerals 1–5 on their footprints. Then, have children place the footprints in numerical order and count them.

Similar numbered patterns can be made from handprints and bare footprints.

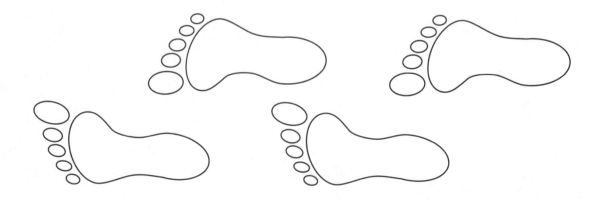

Hide and Tell

Materials: large tray, construction paper, math objects (colorful counters or shapes and numbers)

This activity strengthens visual memory and language development skills. To make the math objects, cut out shapes and numbers from construction paper using the patterns on pages 52–53.

Select five to seven objects to place on the tray. Hold up each object for children to see. Let children describe each object that you hold up. Next, have children close their eyes while you take one object off the tray.

When children open their eyes, have them tell you which object is missing. Repeat this process many times. When you add a new object, be sure to let children describe the object before it goes on the tray. You can also have children count the number of objects on the tray.

Poof Ball Toss

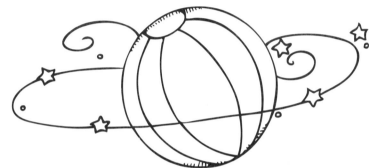

Materials: several soft, lightweight balls such as foam or loofah balls; containers to throw balls into (plastic containers, buckets, shoe boxes, etc.); precut shapes; color strips or numbers; copies of pages 52–53

Make copies of pages 52–53 and cut out the patterns. Determine what areas you want the groups of children to work on—numbers, shapes, or colors. Tape whatever you decide to work on the containers. (Example: shapes—Tape a shape from page 52 to each container.)

Set up the containers inside or outside the school. Give each child some foam balls to hold. Have children come up to the boxes and tell you which one they are aiming for. Let them try to throw their foam balls into the container. Then, let them try again for the same number, shape, or color or tell you a different target choice.

If necessary, make a tape or string line for children to stand on to determine throwing distance. You may leave this activity up all day for the children to play.

Shape Patterns

Number Patterns

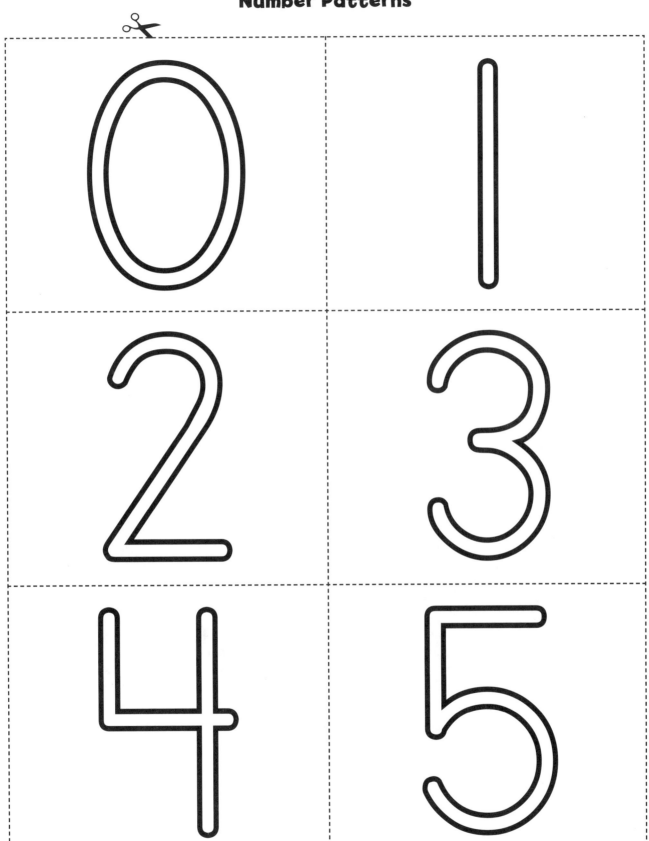

53

Bears in Chairs

Materials: children's chairs, teddy bears, children's books (one item per child, and if possible, an equal number of each)

This one-to-one correspondence activity brings smiles to the teddy bear lovers in your class. Each child chooses a chair or a bear or a book. The "chair" children start by placing their chairs in a straight line. They step back to the circle and lead the group in counting the chairs. The "bear" children place one bear in each chair and return to the circle. They lead the group in counting the bears. The "book" children place one book in the lap of each teddy bear and lead the group in counting the books. All of the children then chant together, for example, "Five bears in five chairs read five books."

Color Run

Materials: construction paper, cut into small squares

Children learn best when using their bodies. This activity reinforces colors through running and stopping. Tape a small color tag on each child. Use a variety of colors. Then call out, for example, "Everyone with a red tag can run." After children do a short run, blow the whistle for the red tag children to sit or "freeze." Repeat this activity until all of the children have had a turn. Try taping two or three different colors on each child so that the children have to double-check to see if they have the color that you called out. As children learn to play, use a variety of motor skills. Yellow tag children can hop, blue tag children can crawl, and green tag children can walk fast, etc.

Hop on Colors

Materials: construction paper

Children follow directions, learn to hop, and reinforce color recognition in this activity. Place different colors of construction paper all over the floor. Make sure that you have three or four sheets of each color or enough rectangles on the floor for all of the children. Tell the children to move from rectangle to rectangle by hopping. Call out, for example, "John, hop to a blue rectangle," "Sue, hop to a yellow rectangle," etc. Another variation is to place white construction paper on the floor. Then, place different colors under each of the white rectangles. Let children hop from one to the next. When you signal them to stop hopping, have each child pick up the white rectangle on which she landed and name the color that is under the white rectangle.

People, Places, and Things

Materials: magazines, manila envelopes, poster board, index cards

Recognizing similarities and differences and classifying are important science skills. This activity helps young children develop all of these skills. Look through magazines to collect a variety of interesting pictures. As you collect the pictures, categorize them according to topic. Manila envelopes work well for this purpose. You might start with five or six categories, such as people, transportation, animals, plants, houses, and toys. Look for pictures of all sizes. Glue large pictures onto sheets of poster board and smaller ones onto index cards.

Once you have collected a number of pictures in each category, use them to explore similarities and differences with the children. For example, show the children eight or 10 dog pictures. Have them think of ways the dogs are the same and ways the dogs are different. Let them decide how to categorize the dogs—by size, by color, or by type; by whether the dog is wearing a collar; or by some other criteria. Repeat with other sets of pictures. Encourage children to think of a range of ways to sort each group. For example, they could sort pictures of people by age or facial expression or by whether they are sitting or standing. They could sort pictures of houses by color, size, or number of windows, or by whether they have chimneys.

What Is the Weather?

Materials: magazines

Learning about the weather can be fun when music and movement are involved. Cut out magazine pictures that depict sunny, rainy, snowy, and windy weather and show them to the children. Ask children to tell you what kinds of activities they can do outside in each kind of weather and what kind of clothing they should wear. Then, sing the following song. Have children shout out the kind of weather needed for that activity at the end of each verse. If you wish, let children make up additional verses.

Sing to the tune of: "Do You Know the Muffin Man?"

When you build a great snowman,
A great snowman, a great snowman,
When you build a great snowman,
What is the weather?

When you splash in mud puddles,
In mud puddles, in mud puddles,
When you splash in mud puddles,
What is the weather?

When you build a sand castle,
A sand castle, a sand castle,
When you build a sand castle,
What is the weather?

When you fly a super kite,
A super kite, a super kite,
When you fly a super kite,
What is the weather?

Gayle Bittinger

The Wind Is Moving Air

Materials: balloon, bottle of bubbles, straw, glass of water, candle

The following activities involve teacher demonstration using materials not appropriate for young children to handle. Explaining the properties of wind to young children is not an easy task. Tell children that the wind is air. You can't see air. But, air is all around you—above you, behind you, and in front of you. Even though you can't see the air, you can see what the air does and how it feels. Try these demonstrations:

Balloon: Air is what is inside a balloon when you blow it up. Air comes out of the balloon when you let it go.

Soap bubbles: Air is what is inside a soap bubble. Blow some bubbles with the children.

Straw and bubbles: When you blow through a straw into a glass of water, it is the air that makes bubbles.

Candle: It is the air that blows out a candle.

 **(See page 2.)**

(See page 2.)

Making a Cloud

Materials: glass jar, hot water, crushed ice

This activity involves teacher demonstration using materials not appropriate for young children to handle. Pour hot water into a glass jar. When the bottle becomes hot, pour out all but one inch of the water. Stretch a cloth over the mouth of the jar. Fasten. Place some crushed ice on top of the cloth. A cloud forms as the warm air meets the cold. Discuss the difference between hot and cold.

Sprouting Carrots

Materials: carrots, knife, dishes, pebbles, water

Growing plants in the classroom is a great way for children to experience living things in their environment. Cut off some carrot tops and place each one in a dish with pebbles. Add just enough water to cover the bottom of the carrot. Place the dishes in an area that is not too sunny. In just a few days, the carrot tops will begin to sprout and turn into beautiful plants.

A Pretty Plant

Materials: pineapple, knife, bowl, water, pot with dirt, plastic bag

In the spring, many farmers and gardeners begin to prepare for the planting season. Here is an exciting activity for preschool children—growing a pineapple plant.

Bring a pineapple to school. Let children watch you cut it and share the fun of eating it. Cut off the top of the pineapple, leaving about one inch of the fruit. Place the pineapple top in water, leaving the leaves exposed to the air. Within 2–3 weeks when roots appear, transfer the plant to a pot of dirt and cover with a plastic bag for three weeks. After everyone has waited patiently for the three weeks to pass, remove the cover. You will discover a pretty cactus-like plant. Uncovering the plant and seeing how it has grown is amazing to young children.

How Do Plants Grow?

Materials: resealable plastic bags, water, flower or vegetable seeds, paper towels

Children will enjoy growing plants inside the classroom. Place assorted seeds between paper towels inside a resealable plastic bag. Pour enough water into the plastic bag to saturate the paper towel. Seal the top of the bag and place it in a sunny place. The seeds will soon start to grow. Tell children that the roots will grow toward the water, and the stems will grow toward the sunlight. Compare the growth of the different plants daily. To continue plant growth, transfer the plants to pots of dirt.

Habitat Game

Materials: poster board, markers, magazines

Set out three sheets of poster board and draw a different animal habitat (sky, ocean, forest) on each one. Look through magazines to find pictures of animals that live in these habitats. Place the habitat posters in the middle of the circle. Let children take turns choosing an animal picture and placing it on the habitat where it lives. Sing the following song when all of the animal pictures are in their habitats:

Sing to the tune of: "Twinkle, Twinkle, Little Star."

In the ocean you will find
Animals of every kind.
Sharks and fish and dolphins too,
Octopus and whales of blue.
In the ocean you will find
Animals of every kind.
In the blue sky you will find
Animals of every kind.
Robins, bats, and bald eagles,
Hummingbirds and gray seagulls.
In the blue sky you will find
Animals of every kind.

In the forest you will find
Animals of every kind.
Bears and deer and ringed raccoons.
Timber wolves howling at the moon.
In the forest you will find
Animals of every kind.

Gayle Bittinger

Everyone Needs a Home

Materials: one copy of Animals and Their Homes cut apart, page 59

Note: Use with an even-numbered group of 12 or fewer (or make additional pairs).

Learning about animals is very engaging for young children. Turn pictures facedown in the middle of the floor at circle time. Have each child take one picture.

Ask each child with an animal picture to name the animal. Have children with animal home pictures show their cards. The child with the animal picture decides which illustration shows the appropriate home for that animal.

Have children place the animal and animal home pairs together in the middle of the circle.

Talk about why different animals live in different types of homes.

Animals and Their Homes

  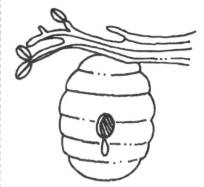

  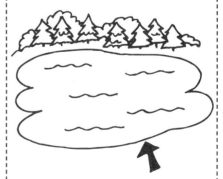

Awesome Animals

Materials: one copy of the animal cards (pages 62 and 63) per child, one copy of the category board (page 61) per child, small toy animals if available (zoo animals, farm animals, reptiles, birds, butterflies), magazines with pictures of land, water, and air creatures

Discuss with children and identify which animals live on land, which ones live in water, and which ones fly. Show children some pictures of these animals.

If possible, take children for a walk or go out on the playground and find some animals that fit into the categories you are discussing.

Give each child a copy of the category board and the animal cards. Have them cut the animal cards apart. Let children categorize the animals into the three categories on the board. Then, let them use toy animals to place on their boards.

For more fun, have children cut animals out of magazines and place them on their category boards.

Air	Water	Land

Land	
Water	
Air	

Animal Cards

Animal Cards

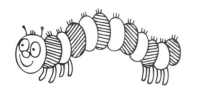

Properties

Talk about the properties or attributes of different objects. Introduce children to descriptive words such as soft, hard, rough, cold, hot, small, empty, and full. Ask them to think of other words that can be used to describe something. Then, name a property and have children think of things that have that property. For example, if you said the property "red," the children could name objects such as a stop sign, a fire truck, a crayon, an apple, a marker, a shirt, and a car.

To make this a hands-on activity, name a property and have children walk around the room to find objects with that property. As each child finds one, have him place the object in the middle of the circle and sit down. After everyone is finished, examine each object to determine how it has that particular property.

Light Show

Materials: flashlights, cellophane, tape or rubber band

Collect several flashlights and a few different colors of cellophane. (Colorful cellophane is available where gift wrap is sold.) Cut circles out of several different colors of cellophane. Tape or rubber band the cellophane circles over the ends of the flashlights, leaving one flashlight uncovered. Have children sit in a circle. Switch on the flashlights and choose several children to hold them. Turn out the room lights. Ask children to observe the lights coming from the various flashlights. What colors of light do they see? Ask them to find out what happens when two lights of different colors shine on the same spot. Have children who are holding the flashlights hand them to someone else. Continue experimenting with the flashlights until each child has had a turn to hold one.

Sorting Hard and Soft

Materials: soft objects such as feathers, ribbons, scarves, cotton, tissue, leaves, flower petals; hard objects such as wood, stones, paper clips, toothpicks; two index cards; two sheets of construction paper

In this activity, children will sort hard and soft objects. Write *soft* on one index card and *hard* on the other. Discuss the meaning of the words *soft* and *hard* with the children. Let the children feel some soft and hard objects.

Place a variety of objects on a table for children to classify as hard or soft. Place the hard and soft word cards above sheets of construction paper. Encourage children to identify and place each object on the appropriate sheet of construction paper. You may give the objects to each child in a bag or have the children work in groups to select and place objects from the table.

 **(See page 2.)**

Rough or Smooth?

Materials: box filled with various materials that are rough or smooth such as sandpaper, cotton, silk, nylon, crumpled foil, wood block, etc.

Children learn more when all of their senses are involved. The focus of this activity is on the sense of touch. Ask children to shut their eyes and then feel the materials. They should describe the textures using the words *rough* and *smooth*.

Loud and Soft Sounds

Materials: CD player, CDs of various music

This activity uses auditory discrimination games with music and sound. Children enjoy listening to CDs or recordings of various sounds. Play the sounds loudly and softly and have children identify which are loud and which are soft.

Children may also enjoy making their own recordings of loud and soft sounds.

Alive vs. Not Alive

In many stories and fairy tales, children are exposed to a variety of objects that are not alive but do and say things as if they were alive. For example, brooms may dance, cookies may jump out of ovens, and furniture may talk. Discuss with children things that are not alive—chairs, tables, stuffed animals, etc. What makes something alive? (It breathes, eats, etc.) What is alive in your classroom, and what is not alive?

Comparing Rocks

Materials: assortment of rocks, nail

Discuss safety and careful use of materials before starting this activity. Have children compare the rocks, looking at several different features:

1. Is this rock hard or soft? Can you scratch it with a nail?
2. What color is the rock?
3. How big is the rock?
4. Is the rock rough or smooth?
5. What shape is the rock?

 (See page 2.)

Magnets

Materials: large and small magnets; variety of small objects such as paper clips, nails, buttons, bottle caps, wooden beads; construction paper; glass of water

Children are fascinated by activities that use magnets. Allow children to experiment with the small objects and the magnets. Which ones will the magnet pick up? Arrange the paper clips on the sheet of construction paper. Let children move a magnet under the paper. What happens? Place the paper clips in a glass of water. Have children move a magnet around the outside of the glass. What happens? Place a large magnet and a small magnet the same distance from an object that will be attracted. Move the magnets closer to the object. Compare the distance at which the object will be attracted. Give each child a magnet and have children find things in the room that the magnets will attract.

 (See page 2.)

Making Dolls Dance

Materials: cardboard box, clear cellophane folder cover, string of paper dolls cut slightly smaller than the depth of the box, handkerchief or tissue

Read the following explanation of electricity to the children:

Electricity is very important. All kinds of things in our homes use electricity: lamps, washing machines, stoves, TVs, and phones. Electricity can help keep us warm in the winter and cool in the summer.

There are two kinds of electricity. The kind that we just talked about is called "current" electricity. It is extremely dangerous. Children should not play with things that use current electricity, such as lamps, TVs, and washing machines.

The other kind of electricity is called "static" electricity. This is not as dangerous. Static electricity happens when two things rub against each other. We are going to do an experiment where you will see how static electricity can make paper dolls dance.

Cut the clear cellophane folder cover to make a cover for the box. Stand the dolls up in the box. Cover the cardboard box with the cellophane lid. Rub the top of the box with the handkerchief or tissue. The dolls will "dance" because of the static electricity created by the rubbing.

Floating Fish

Materials: water table or plastic bin, card stock, vegetable oil

Here is a fun experiment that will actually make a fish move in water. Cut a sheet of card stock into the shape of a fish. Cut a slit in the tail of the fish. Punch a hole at the end of the slit, and add a drop of cooking oil in this hole. Place the fish on the surface of the water. The fish will move forward under its own power.

Walking Tour

Gather children in a circle and talk about walking. What do we use to walk with? How many different ways of walking can the children come up with?

Invite children to go on a walking tour with you around your circle. Have them listen carefully and follow your directions as you walk together.

It's time to take a circle walk. Let's start out with big steps.

Now, take even bigger steps.

Now, take teeny, tiny steps.

Now, try walking on your tiptoes.

Now, let's hold hands while we walk.

Now, let's drop our hands and walk.

Now, pretend you're walking up a hill.

Now, down a hill.

Now, let's walk like the hands of a clock.

Now, let's walk in the opposite direction.

Now, let's walk sideways.

Now, let's walk backward.

Now, bend over and stretch your legs after all of that walking.

Footprints

Materials: short crepe paper streamers, several footprint shapes in two colors. (Make all of the left-foot shapes one color and the right-foot shapes another color.)

This simple movement activity helps reinforce the concept of left and right. Tape the footprint shapes to the floor in a walking pattern in a circle around the room. Using crepe paper streamers in the two colors that match the footprints, tape different-colored bands to the ankles of each child. The left bands should match the color of the left footprints, and the right bands should match the color of the right footprints. As children walk around the circle on the footprints, have them match their bands to the color of the prints. Call out the names of the colors to help them match their gait. For example, if the right-foot color is red and the left-foot color is blue, say, "Red, blue, red, blue," etc.

Learning the Ropes

Materials: fabric jump ropes

Coordination, balance, and jumping help children's confidence grow as they practice all of the skills in these jump rope activities.

Extend a jump rope on the floor for a safe and easy "balance beam". As children explore it for the first time, they may want to walk on or along it, or jump over it. Let them try out any safe ideas. As children become more comfortable, try these variations:

Circus Performers
Have children pretend they are tightrope performers as they practice walking on the line. Have them walk slowly at first and then faster as they are able.

Backward Walkers
Let children try walking backward along the rope. Have them pay attention to the rope under their feet to tell them where to step next.

Snake Walk
Lay the jump rope in a curvy pattern. Have children follow the curves as they walk along the rope.

Jumping the tracks
Lay two ropes parallel, about 12 inches (30.5 cm) apart, on the floor to make "railroad tracks". Have children try jumping inside the tracks, outside the tracks, and on the tracks.

Follow the Leader
Choose one child to be the leader. Have the leader walk across the rope in two or three different ways. Let the other children follow her movements. Have children take turns being the leader. If you wish, help the leader sing the following song while the children follow her across the jump rope.

> *Sing to the tune of: "Frère Jacques"*
>
> Follow me, follow me.
> If you please, if you please.
> Watch and do what I do,
> Watch and do what I do.
> Follow me, follow me.
>
> *Gayle Bittinger*

Rope Swing
Select a helper to hold one end of the rope while you gently swing the other. Have the children jump one at a time, over the moving rope. As the children gain confidence, raise the rope a bit off the ground for the children to jump over. Wiggling the rope is another fun way to vary this activity.

 **(See page 2.)**

1-2-3-4-5

This is a fun rhyme for exercising. When practicing for a "Preschool Olympics" or a "Track and Field Day," this rhyme can provide a good warm-up activity.

> Hands on shoulders,
> Hands on knees,
> Hands on head,
> 1-2-3.
>
> Hands on nose,
> Hands on ears,
> Hands on the floor,
> 1-2-3-4.
>
> Hands in front,
> Hands to the side,
> Hands in the sky,
> 1-2-3-4-5.

Follow the Leader

Have children line up directly behind you. Have them stand at least an arm's length apart. Start to walk around the room, moving in different patterns and assuming various body positions.

Jumping the Brook

Materials: masking tape; pictures of waterfalls, brooks, and other small bodies of water

Have children share their experiences with bodies of water as you share pictures of local or faraway places. Then, make X's on the floor with tape to make the "rocks" in the "brook." Place them in random sequence, varying the distance apart.

1. Have children take turns jumping with feet together from "rock" to "rock," landing on each X with both feet.

2. Next, have them jump and straddle the X's with both feet.

3. Last, have them jump from X to X, alternating takeoff with the right foot and then the left foot.

Safety First! (See page 2.)

Roll-a-Ball

Materials: chalk, playground ball

Children will be challenged as they learn to control how hard or softly they roll the ball. Use chalk to draw a large circle on the floor. Draw a line several feet from the circle. Have children stand behind the line and take turns trying to roll the ball into the circle. If the ball does not roll into the circle or if it rolls out, tell the child to sit.

Moving Like Animals

Moving like animals integrates science and gross motor skills into fun activities for young children. Give children instructions for each of these activities.

Bear Walk
Place your hands on the floor in front of you and take giant bear steps with your hands and feet. Remember to growl like a bear. Keep a nose out for juicy berries.

Bunny Hop
While standing, bend your arms and let your wrists flop in front of your chest. Hop, hop, hop to the carrot patch.

Camel Walk
Place your hands on the floor in front of you and try to keep your legs stiff as you lead the caravan through the desert. Stop at the nearest oasis for a drink of water.

Frog Jump
Squat with knees out and place your hands on the floor between your knees. Jump up and down in this position. Once you have the technique, hunt for some insects. Remember to *ribbit* and catch insects with your tongue.

Crab Walk
Sit on the floor, place your hands behind you, bend your knees, and keep your feet flat on the floor. Now, lift your bottom off the floor. Try to keep your stomach flat. Crabs mostly move sideways, but they can also move forward and backward.

Horse Kick
Squat and place your hands on the floor in front of you. Kick your legs behind you. Try one leg at a time and then both at once. (Be sure to support your weight on your arms and don't kick too high, or you might fall.) *Whinny* like a horse and watch out for breakable objects or furniture. Make sure that children have enough room to move safely.

 **(See page 2.)**

Whooo Is Calling?

Listening to sounds without visual cues can be challenging for young children. While children are sitting in a circle, place a chair in front of the group with its back to children. Choose one child to be the first to sit in the chair. Explain that you will point to a child in the group. That child will say, "*Whooo!*" like an owl. The child sitting in the chair will try to guess who is making the sound. Allow children to take turns being the owl and the guesser.

Bunny Number Hop

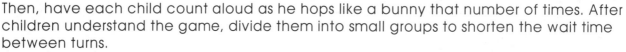

Materials: dice or a larger die made from a small square box

Children will enjoy hopping like bunnies. Gather children and explain that they will play a counting and hopping game. Allow one child at a time to roll a die and count the number of dots. Then, have each child count aloud as he hops like a bunny that number of times. After children understand the game, divide them into small groups to shorten the wait time between turns.

Bear Cave Hide

Materials: at least one medium- to large-sized box per child (boxes should be large enough for a child to fit in)

Pretending to be animals inspires creative thinking and enthusiastic participants. Have children help you spread the boxes throughout the playground, with the openings facing to the side. Tell children that these boxes are "bear caves." Tell children that they will walk or run around the playground until you whistle. When they hear the whistle, they are to run and hide in one of the bear caves. This game has no winners or losers—everyone finds a cave!

The Bunny Hop

Have children move around the room like bunnies. Then, teach them how to dance the Bunny Hop. Tell them to turn so that they are facing the back of the person in front of them. Have them place their hands on each other's shoulders as if they were linking up to form a choo-choo train. Then, have everyone balance on one foot while tapping the other one to the side, shift balance and tap the opposite foot, repeat the foot taps on both sides, and then hop forward three times. Tell them to continue these steps as they move around in a circle. If you wish, make up a hopping song to sing as children do the Bunny Hop. Talk about other animals that hop, such as frogs and kangaroos. How might a dance called the Kangaroo Hop differ from the Bunny Hop?

Hop Like the Animals

Talk with children about animals that get from one place to another by hopping. Bring in books about these animals to share with children. Explore what it might be like to hop around all of the time. How might you eat breakfast while hopping? How might you comb your hair?

Little Birds

The birds are returning home from the south. Have children be the birds. They should do what the rhymes tell them. Make up other rhymes to fit your location.

1. Little birds, little birds
   Fly to the door.
   Little birds, little birds
   Sit on the floor.

2. Little birds, little birds
   Jump up and down.
   Little birds, little birds
   Don't make a sound.

3. Little birds, little birds
   Tiptoe to me.
   Little birds, little birds
   Sit down on your knees.

4. Little birds, little birds
   Creep, creep, creep.
   Little birds, little birds
   Sleep, sleep, sleep.

The Duck Family

Have children act out the following story as you read it. They may want to do this several times.

THE STORY: A mother duck and three baby ducks were taking a nap. (You may use the entire class instead of three baby ducks.) One duck awoke and paddled away—then another—then another. Mother woke up. She quacked loudly. The babies answered their mother, and the mother duck found them by their sounds. (The babies quack softly until they are found.)

Duck Waddle Relay Race

Although relay races are sometimes complicated for young children, this one will be fun. Divide the class into three or four equal groups and line up children by group. Tell children that they will race like ducks. When you signal, have the first student in each group waddle to a marked point and return to her team and tag the next student in line. After the second student is tagged, she will waddle as the first child did. The first team to finish wins.

Find Your Partner

Materials: pictures of zoo animals

Tape a picture of a zoo animal on each child. For example, if you have 10 children in your class, use five different animals (two pictures of each) so that each child has a match. Have one child at a time skip, hop, or jump around the room until she hears you say, "Go find your partner." She will stop beside the child who is wearing the same animal picture and take the partner's hand. Then, they will go around the room together. When they have finished their turn, choose another child to go find his partner.

Cat Warm-up

Talk about cats with children. If you wish, bring in pictures of different cat breeds or picture books with stories and pictures of cats. Then, have children imitate cat movements. Ask them to show how cats walk, play with a ball of string, curl up in front of a warm fire, or drink a bowl of milk. Have them pretend to be cats that are happy, afraid, angry, or hungry.

Rocking Horses

Have children lie on the floor and pretend to be rocking horses. Show them how to pull their knees as close to their chins as possible. Then, tell them to wrap their arms around their legs and rock back and forth. This stretch is not only fun but is soothing to the muscles in the upper back.

Safety First! (See page 2.)

Favorite Pets

This version of Follow the Leader allows children to be creative in their dramatic play. Select one child to be the leader. Have her stand in the middle of the circle. The leader must tell the group what type of animal she is looking for. One by one, the children in the circle can pretend to be that animal. Have each child move around and make the noise the animal would make. The leader chooses the "animal" she wants. Then, that child becomes the new leader, choosing a different kind of pet.

Tiptoe Chase

Materials: masking tape or string

Children love to tiptoe in this "sleepy" chasing activity. Divide children in the circle into "cats" and "dogs." Using tape or string, mark one line at one end of the classroom and a second line at the other. Have the cats wait behind the first line while the dogs pretend to be asleep behind the other. Then, let the cats tiptoe silently toward the dogs. When you say, "Chase!" the dogs should wake up and chase the cats. The cats must then race back behind the cat line. Any tagged cats must join the dogs. Switch roles so that the dogs tiptoe toward the cats. Continue while interest lasts. Move this game outdoors if you need more room.

Cattle Call

Have children pretend to be cows running and grazing around the pasture (the classroom or the circle). As the farmer, your job is to herd the cows into groups of two to six cows to return them to the barn. If you pick two, for example, call out, "Two by two." The cows must then scramble to line up in groups of two. Any cows left grazing will line up with you. Give children the opportunity to take turns being the farmer. Change the type of farm animal being herded. Geese, chickens, goats, sheep, and horses are just a few examples.

Slippery Fish

Form a large circle with half of the children in your group. (You may want to have them take a giant step backward so that the circle is even larger.) Invite the children in the circle to pretend to be fish with big "jaw" arms. Encourage the rest to pretend to be swimmers. When you say, "Jaws open," the fish should hold hands and lift them overhead while the swimmers "swim" freely through the circle. When you say, "Slippery fish," the fish should lower their jaws and run in a circle while the swimmers "swim" out of the circle. Swimmers caught inside the circle become slippery fish. Have the groups switch roles periodically.

Cobra Stretches

Stretches are relaxing and calming for young children. Have children lie on their stomachs with their arms underneath their chests. Their hands should be palms down. Show children how to use their arms to raise their upper bodies so that they resemble cobras raising their hoods to strike. Make sure that they don't arch their backs too far—this should be a comfortable stretch. Their legs should not move. If you wish, have children wag their tongues in and out of their mouths like snakes.

Have one child sit in the middle of the circle and pretend to be a snake charmer while the "cobras" stretch. If you wish, provide the snake charmer with a rhythm instrument to play while the children are stretching.

Upside-Down Snake Stretches

Stretches and poses are good to do as a transition to quiet time or story time. Have children sit on the floor with their legs extended and their arms resting on the floor slightly behind their hips. Next, have them lift their bottoms toward the ceiling, keeping their heels on the ground. Tell them to tilt their heads back and hold the stretch as long as possible. What other animal might move like this? Why?

Snake in a Tunnel

Young children enjoy the motor skill of crawling. Crawling is especially fun when they have something to crawl through. Provide children with things to crawl through, such as an open-ended large box or a barrel. Or, use sheets or blankets to cover tables and chairs.

Have children pretend that they are a snake and that they are crawling through a tunnel. Tell them to try not to touch the sides of the tunnel as they crawl through it.

Chicken, Chicken, Who Has Your Egg?

Materials: plastic egg

Children love this guessing game. Choose one child to be the chicken. Have him sit with his back to the class with a plastic egg behind him. Tell children that you will tap one person on the shoulder. That person should quietly sneak up behind the "chicken," take the egg, and then return to his seat and hide the egg in his lap. Encourage children to hide their hands as if they have the egg. After children are ready, they ask, "Chicken, chicken, who has your egg?" The chicken turns around, surveys the class, and guesses who has the egg. He is allowed three guesses. If he does not guess correctly, the child with the egg becomes the next chicken. If he does guess correctly, he gets another turn.

Ball Butting

Take extra care that children safely use their heads in this activity. Discuss how goats butt objects with their heads. Explain that male goats do this when they are young to show who is the strongest. Tell children that they will pretend to be goats by butting balls with their heads. Use beach balls or other lightweight balls. Divide the class into groups of two to four, depending on the number of balls you have, and allow one child to gently pitch the ball in the direction of the others and have the others butt it back. Be sure to tell students that the balls are the only things they are allowed to butt with their heads!

Hoops of Fun

Materials: large plastic hoops, paper bags

Collect several plastic hoops in various sizes. Use the hoops in the following activities to help children develop their gross motor skills.

Five Is Still Five

Give each child a paper bag to carry on a nature walk. Ask each child to pick up five objects to place in the bag along the way (twig, acorn, pine cone, etc.). In a large space inside or outdoors, have each child place a large hoop on the floor, empty the objects from the bag inside the hoop, and count the objects. Ask children, "Do you have five? Give directions such as, "Move all of your nature items to the middle of the hoop and count them," or "Place all of your nature items in a straight line in the hoop and count them." No matter how the children place the items, five is still five!

Hoop Commands

Give each child a hoop. Have children place their hoops on the floor. Ask them to jump inside their hoops, outside their hoops, and around their hoops. Have them hold their hoops above their heads and sit in the middle of their hoops. If you wish, let children take turns giving hoop commands to each another.

Ride around the Hoop

Have all of the children hold onto one large toy hoop as you sing the following song. (If all of the children cannot fit around one hoop, divide them into smaller groups and use two or more hoops.)

Sing to the tune of: "Ring Around the Rosy."

Riding around the big hoop (Hold onto hoop as you circle around.)
On our frisky ponies.
Buck once, buck twice—(Lift up hoop at the word *buck*.)
We all fall down. (Let go of hoop and fall down.)

Virginia Colvig

Moving with Carpet Squares

Materials: carpet squares

Check a local carpet store for sample squares of discontinued carpet styles. You can also make your own carpet squares by cutting large scraps of carpet into 2-foot (0.6-m) squares.

Carpet squares are great tools for developing young children's motor skills. Collect at least one carpet square for each child. Then, try the following games:

Magic Carpet Rides
Give each child a carpet square to sit on. Invite children to go on a "magic carpet ride." Let them spread their arms to make "wings," and have them lean one way and then the other. Encourage them to tell what they "see" on their imaginary carpet rides.

Frog Jump
Scatter carpet squares around the room. Have each child pretend to be a frog and crouch down on one of the carpet squares. Let children practice making frog jumps off of their carpet square "lily pads." Encourage them to *ribbit* as they jump.

Follow the Leader
Arrange carpet squares in a line, keeping them about 6" apart. Choose one child to be the leader. Have the other children follow the leader as he or she jumps, hops, walks backward, or tiptoes down the line of carpet squares. Let children take turns being the leader.

Follow Directions
Place carpet squares in a circle on the floor. Have each child sit on a carpet square. Give children simple directions to follow. For example, ask children to stand with both feet on their squares, jump up and down on their squares, or touch their squares with their hands. As children become more experienced in following directions, give them multiple-step directions. For example, ask children to stand on carpet squares and turn around, jump on their carpet squares and clap their hands, or stand with one foot on their carpet squares while they wave and blink.

Parachute Fun

Materials: parachute

Have children hold a parachute by the edges.
As you sing the following song, have them raise
the parachute above their heads so that it billows
like a big tent. Call out each child's name one
by one. As you say a child's name, have him
run under the parachute and grab hold of it on
the other side. Then, tell children to slowly lower
the parachute. Continue playing until all of the
children have had a chance to run.

Sing to the tune of: "Row, Row, Row Your Boat."

Up, up, up it goes.
Down, down, down it comes.
If your name is _____,
Now's your turn to run!

Diane Thom

Sing the following song while children raise and lower the parachute. Have them stomp
their feet each time the parachute goes up as mentioned in the song. Encourage
children to think of other movements to substitute for stomping their feet.

Sing to the tune of: "If You're Happy and You Know It."

When the parachute goes up,
Stomp your feet.
When the parachute goes up,
Stomp your feet.
When the parachute is high,
It floats up to the sky.
When the parachute goes up,
Stomp your feet.

Diane Thom

Balance Beam Skills

Materials: balance beam or construction/butcher paper, tape, ruler, colorful objects, two balls

Give these directions to the children:

1. Walk forward, toes pointed straight ahead, eyes looking down, heel in front of the toe.
2. Walk the same style as above but with eyes looking straight ahead.
3. Walk forward to the middle, turn, and walk back.
4. Walk backward, using arms as balancing rods.
5. Hop on one foot.
6. Jump on the beam, landing with one foot in front of the other each time.
7. Stand on one leg and swing the other leg back and forth.
8. Sit on the beam with feet straight out.
9. Sit with knees bent and then with knees straight.
10. Walk with weight on all fours like an animal; first, walk forward with hands while keeping feet in place; then, walk feet up to meet hands.
11. Bounce a ball while walking; then, try bouncing two balls.
12. Throw the ball into the air and catch it while walking.

Balance Beam Color Land

After practicing the above balance beam activities, children will be ready for this more challenging activity. Gather colorful objects that children can pick up when they are on the balance beam. Be sure the objects are safe and easy to pick up (plastic cars, plastic animals, math manipulatives, etc.). Set up the balance beam in your classroom. If you do not have a balance beam, you can make one from construction paper or butcher paper by cutting the paper 4" by 12" (10.16 cm x 30.48 cm) long and taping it to the floor. (If children have never had the experience of using a balance beam, be sure to do the tape balance beam first.) Place the objects within easy reach along the length of the beam.

Let one child go across the balance beam and tell him to pick up a specific object. He must try to pick up the object without placing his feet on the floor and continue to cross the beam.

When the child is at the end of the balance beam, he may want to go to the end of the line to wait for another turn.

 **(See page 2.)**

Mashed Potatoes

Children will enjoy waiting and listening for the "signal" to wiggle. Stand in the middle of the circle and let children hop all around as you name favorite foods such as hamburgers, cheese, apples, pizza, salad, celery, and macaroni and cheese. Have children listen for the words *mashed potatoes*. When you say, "Mashed potatoes!" it is their cue to drop to the floor and wiggle around. Invite other children to take your place in the middle of the circle and name their favorite foods.

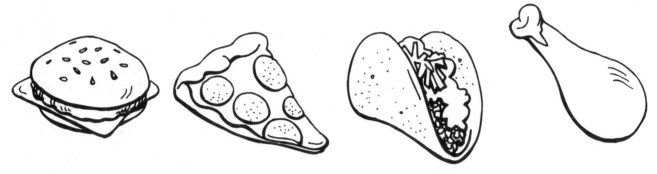

Applesauce

Explain to children that the circle is a magic kettle and that they are apples in the pot. Tell them that they are being made into applesauce. Have everyone move to the center of the "pot" and begin gently bumping into each other, rolling around, and bobbing up and down like apples cooking in a pot. Periodically, call out, "Applesauce!" Whenever you do so, have children give a huge group hug. Then, have children resume the gentle bumping, rolling, and bobbing.

Paper Trail

Materials: construction paper cut into different shapes

Arrange different shapes of colorful paper on the floor, leaving about 6 inches (15.24 cm) between each sheet. (You may want to tape them in place.) Have children line up and follow you as you hop from one shape to the next. Lead them to practice hopping forward, backward, and sideways. Have them try hopping on one foot. If you wish, let children take turns being the leader.

Street Sweepers

Have children stand with one foot on the ground and one foot raised approximately 3 inches (7.62 cm) to the side. Instruct them to keep their hands on their hips for balance. Now, have them "sweep" their legs by hopping from one foot to the other. Show them how to slightly bend the supporting leg to protect their knees.

Hot Potato

Hot Potato is a perennial favorite because it is so simple and fun to play. Pass a small ball or beanbag around the circle. Invite children to pretend it is a real baked potato hot from the oven. They will need to pass it quickly around the circle to avoid "burning" their fingers. If you wish, play music as the children pass the "hot potato." When the music stops, the person left holding it gets to select the music for the next round.

Theme Potato
Build upon a current theme your class is studying. For example, if you are investigating dinosaurs, have children pass around a small bone or dinosaur toy. If you are learning about squares, pass around a square-shaped item. This activity works especially well for holiday, color, and sensory themes too.

Snack Potato
Pass around a granola bar or other packaged snack. When the music stops, the child left holding the snack gets to keep it. Repeat with a new snack. Play this a few times before giving a snack to everyone.

Surprise Potato
Pass around a box with a lid. The child left holding the box gets to guess what's inside. Then, that child can peek inside and check her guess. If the guess is incorrect, she can then give the group one hint about the object before the game continues.

Adjective Potato
Pretend that the "potato" is sticky, slimy, cold, sharp, or soft. How does this affect how the children pass it to each other? Think of other words to use in place of *hot*.

Cuddly Potato
Pass around something cuddly, such as a blanket or stuffed animal. The child left holding it gets a group hug.

Over and Under

Materials: playground or smaller balls

Children will have fun learning the concepts of "over" and "under" in this activity. Arrange children in the circle so that they are facing the back of the person in front of them. Have them stand in the circle with their legs apart. Demonstrate how to bend at the waist and pass a playground or smaller ball through their legs to the person behind them. Let the children pass the ball around the circle this way. Then, show them how to pass the ball over their heads to the person behind them. As before, continue this movement around the circle. For a final challenge, have children alternate passing the ball under and over as it moves around the circle.

Juggling

Materials: several soft, small balls of different colors

This activity will take practice, but children will enjoy the challenge. Have children start passing one ball around the circle. Then, start a ball going the other way, so that two balls are being passed around the circle simultaneously. See how many more balls children can pass around at the same time.

Group Weave

Materials: two different colors of yarn

This activity reinforces cooperation and teamwork. It takes the participation of all hands to keep the weavers moving through the circle. Invite two children to stand outside the circle and pretend to be weavers. Give each "weaver" one very long piece of yarn. Have children in the circle stand with their arms straight out in front of them with their palms facing up. Let the "weavers" work together to make patterns as they thread the yarn in and out between the children's hands in the circle.

Group Sit

Children will want to do this again and again throughout the school year. Arrange children in the circle so that they are facing the back of the person in front of them. Have children squeeze together as tightly as they can. Then, have everyone sit on the lap of the person in back of him at the count of three. Once you have successfully experienced a group sit, see if the group can move forward while still maintaining a seated position.

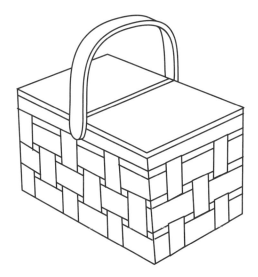

Picnic Lunch

Materials: basket or picnic basket

Imaginative play is important for young children. Encourage imagination in this game of "pretend." Bring a basket to the circle. As you pass the basket around the circle, have each child pretend to take out an item of food or drink. Have children hold up the "food" and tell the group what it is. Encourage children to talk about the size and the texture of the food. How might they hold a cold glass of lemonade differently from a juicy slice of watermelon, a thin peanut butter sandwich, a bunch of grapes, or a large bag of chips? When everyone has some "food," have children begin to "eat." Tell children to think about what it is they are eating as they chew and take bites.

Just Fruity

Have children pretend to be their favorite fruits. Can they peel like a banana, be squishy like grapes, or be crunchy like an apple? Or, are they sticky and juicy like an orange? Encourage children to think about how their favorite fruits smell, look, and feel as they are eaten. Can they think of any other fruits they could pretend to be?

Animal Switch

Materials: pairs of zoo animal pictures from magazines or catalogs

Young children love to learn about large, exotic animals. Some children will be able to share zoo experiences. But for some children, these pictures may be the first time they learn about animals that live in the wild or in a zoo.

Give each student a zoo animal picture and make sure that you give the same animal to two different students. Tell students to listen for the names of their animals or the sounds their animals make. When you say an animal name or imitate an animal's sounds, the two students who are holding the cards of that animal should switch places in the circle. For extra fun, encourage children to make their animals' sounds as they switch places.

Zebra Steps

Materials: string or tape for a starting line and finish line, pictures of zebras

Walking like a four-legged animal is great fun for young children. Show children zebra pictures. Ask children to point out how a zebra looks the same or different from a horse or a donkey. Have children practice walking on all fours. It will take practice! Some children may need to walk on their knees instead of their feet. Have them line up on the starting line. Then, call out different numbers of steps to take. For example, tell children, "Walk three baby zebra steps. Now, walk four big brother zebra steps," etc. Encourage children to continue on all fours until they reach the finish line.

Obstacle Course

This obstacle course provides experience with a variety of gross motor movements and skills.

1. Walk across a balance beam.
2. Climb up on a chair and jump off.
3. Jump through a large hoop with feet together.
4. Crawl under a table.
5. Swing on a rope and jump off.
6. Jump over a box onto a mat.
7. Crawl through a barrel.

Let children add other equipment to the course or exchange something for another piece. Strengthen positional concepts and relationships by using positional words (under the table, over the box, etc.) as children perform the activities.

Flashlight, Flashlight, Where Are You?

Materials: flashlights

When children feel safe in their environment, games and activities in the dark are fun. This activity is good for visual memory and projection as well as peripheral awareness. The idea is to develop rapid movement in the child. Turn the lights off in the gym or the classroom. Tell children to focus their eyes straight ahead. Then, shine a flashlight to the right side of the children. You can flash it a certain number of times or move it in a particular pattern (circle, square, etc.). Have children draw the pattern you flashed or call out the number of times the light flashed. Next, shine the light to the left side of the children and repeat the procedure. For variation, have children repeat the pattern with their own flashlights.

Whistle

Materials: whistle

Children really love this game! It is good for developing motor skills and increasing listening skills.

At a given signal, have children walk in any direction. Tell them that when you blow the whistle, they must stop immediately. Tell children who do not stop on the signal to sit down. Continue until only one child is left. The last player wins the game. Alternate commands you can use are *run*, *crawl*, *skate*, or *tiptoe*.

This is a good game to teach at the beginning of the year. It will teach children that when they hear a whistle, they should stop and listen to you. This will certainly make gathering everyone on the playground a lot easier.

Towel Fun

Materials: bath towels, one per child

This activity allows children to move like frisky squirrels. Tell children that they are squirrels playing outside. Each child should have his own bath towel. Have children spread their towels on the floor and place their hands, feet, and knees at various positions on the towel according to the directions.

1. Put hands in front and feet in back and go forward.
2. Go backward.
3. Put just knees on the towel.
4. Push hands on the towel.
5. Put feet on towel and walk with hands.
6. Ice skate with feet on towel.
7. Put knees on half of the towel and throw arms up to slide forward.
8. Sit in cross-legged position and twist around on towel.

Ladder on the Floor

Materials: ladder or masking tape

Children learn that careful stepping is sometimes important. You can lay a real ladder on the floor or mark a "ladder" on the floor with tape. Tell children that they are firefighters practicing how to use a ladder so that they can help people in tall buildings. Give these directions:

1. Walk forward with one foot on each side of the ladder.
2. Walk forward on the right side of the ladder.
3. Walk forward on the left side of the ladder.
4. Step forward between the rungs of the ladder, alternating your feet.
5. Step backward between the rungs of the ladder, alternating your feet.

The Feather Dance

Materials: feathers

Keeping feathers in the air will provide a fun challenge for young children. Give each child a feather. Show children how to hold the feather in one hand and blow on it to make it float in the air. Challenge children to see how long they can keep their feathers in the air by blowing on them again and again. As children are dancing their "feather dance," sing the following song:

Sing to the tune of "Jingle Bells."

Feather dance, feather dance,
Dancing all around.
Keep your feathers in the air.
Don't let them hit the ground.
Feather dance, feather dance,
Feathers are such fun.
We will dance the feather dance
Until our dance is done.

Gayle Bittinger

If blowing on a feather to keep it in the air is too difficult, let children hold their feathers in their hands and dance around the room while you sing the song.

 **(See page 2.)**

Bubble Wrap Play

Materials: bubble wrap, plastic hammers, masking tape, construction paper

Ask families to donate bubble wrap they have or call local businesses to ask if they have any bubble wrap from packages they've received. You may also purchase bubble wrap at stores that sell shipping supplies. Children love the sound and feel of bubble wrap. Collect sheets of bubble wrap and let the children enjoy the following activities:

Pop It!

Tape bubble wrap to the floor. Let children march, hop, or dance on it to pop the bubbles.

Roll It!

Tape a long sheet of bubble wrap to the floor. Let children take turns rolling like "logs" over the bubbles.

Pound It!

Tape small sheets of bubble wrap to the floor or a table. Let children use plastic hammers to pop the bubbles one at a time. If you wish, place different colors of construction paper under the bubble wrap. Ask the children to pop bubbles over the colors you name.

Squeeze It!

Give each child a small sheet of bubble wrap. While you sing the following song, have children use their fingers to pop the bubbles:

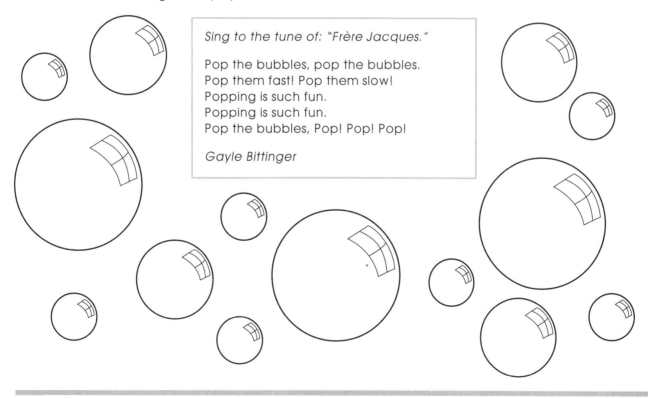

Sing to the tune of: "Frère Jacques."

Pop the bubbles, pop the bubbles.
Pop them fast! Pop them slow!
Popping is such fun.
Popping is such fun.
Pop the bubbles, Pop! Pop! Pop!

Gayle Bittinger

No-Lose Duck, Duck, Goose

This version of Duck, Duck, Goose takes out the frustration of competition among young children. In this activity, every child is a winner. Tell children to spread out in a big circle. Then, have them take two giant steps backward before they sit down. Select one child to be "it." That child will walk around the circle tapping each child lightly on the shoulder and calling out either "duck" or "goose." Remind children in the circle to listen carefully. If the person who is "it" calls out "goose," that child must jump up and honk like a goose. She then changes places with the goose, and the game continues.

Change the name of this game to suit themes or concepts you are working on. For example, if you are teaching about colors, you might call the game Green, Green, Blue. The child tagged as "blue" would then point out something blue in the room. If you are teaching shapes, you might call it Circle, Circle, Square.

Colorful Eggs

Materials: basket filled with colorful plastic eggs

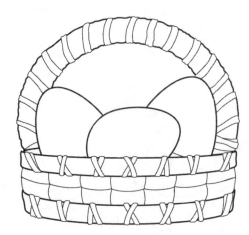

Children will react joyfully every time their color is called by the fox. Designate one child in your circle to be the "fox" while the rest pretend to be "eggs" in a basket. Tell them not to tell anyone what color they are. Then, ask the fox to name an egg color. All eggs of that color must run around the circle and back to their places in the basket before the fox tags them. Any tagged eggs become the fox's helpers. If the fox fails to tag an egg, choose a new fox.

Pass around a basket filled with colorful plastic eggs and have each child choose an egg. The color of egg the children choose will determine what color they will be.

Puddles

Materials: blue construction paper or foil

This is a great activity when a rainy day keeps the children inside. Prepare the same number of puddles as the number of children in the class. Make puddles from blue construction paper or foil. Place them in a circle on the floor. Sing a song about rain. Have children march in a circle, stepping only on the puddles. When the music stops, the children should stop on the puddles. You can also play this game like Musical Chairs. For a different version of this activity, give each child her own puddles. When the music is on, the children walk in a circle around their puddles. When the music stops, the children jump onto their puddles.

Using Our Body Parts

Have children lie on the floor far enough apart so that their hands do not touch when stretched. The children should lie with their feet together, looking at the ceiling, with their hands alongside their bodies. Ask children to relax and to not look at you. Then, lead them in the exercises, doing them slowly. When giving directions, add reference points in the room, such as "the leg nearest the door," "the arm nearest the window," etc.

1. Drag your right hand (add reference point) along the ground until it is pointing above your head. Return your hand to your side.
2. Do the same with your left hand.
3. Move your right leg to the right. Move your leg back.
4. Move your left leg to the left. Move your leg back.
5. Drag both hands on the floor until they touch over your head. Return your hands to your sides.
6. Move both legs apart as far as they can go. Move your legs back.
7. Move your right arm and left leg. Move your arm and leg back.
8. Move your left arm and right leg. Move your arm and leg back.
9. Raise your right arm so that it points at the ceiling. Return your hand to your side.
10. Do the same with your left arm.
11. Raise your right leg toward the ceiling as high as it can go. Move your leg back.
12. Raise your left leg toward the ceiling as high as it can go. Move your leg back.
13. Raise your right arm and right leg as before. Move your arm and leg back.
14. Raise your left arm and left leg as before. Move your arm and leg back.
15. Raise your right arm and left leg. Move your arm and leg back.
16. Raise your left arm and right leg. Move your arm and leg back.

Note: When arms and legs are both moved, they should be moved together.

Build a Tower

Materials: small building blocks, 3–5 for each child

Give each child an equal number of building blocks. Have children sit in a circle with their blocks in front of them. Let them practice building small block towers with their own blocks. Have them notice that the towers are sturdier when the big blocks are on the bottom and the smaller blocks are on the top. Then, explain to children that they

will work together to build a group tower. Choose one child to place the first block in the middle of the circle. Let the other children take turns stacking one block on top of the other to form a tower. Have everyone count as the blocks are added and the tower grows. Continue the game until the tower falls. Then, let the next child start a new tower as everyone begins counting again.

Instead of a tower, let the children build a group structure, such as a castle or a spaceship. Have them continue playing until all of the blocks have been used. When their group structure is complete, sing the following song, substituting the name of their structure for *castle*:

> *Sing to the tune of: "The Hokey Pokey."*
>
> We put the blocks right here.
> We put the blocks right there.
> We put the blocks right here,
> And we gave a little cheer.
> We made a great big castle
> With the help of everyone.
> Building is lots of fun!
>
> *Gayle Bittinger*

Try group tower building using other materials too. Use milk cartons, boxes, dominoes, empty spools, etc. Have each child take a turn placing a block on the tower. See how high the children can build the tower as a group before it falls.

Wake Up, Sleepy Bears

Children will have fun imagining how it would feel to sleep all winter. Have children lie down and pretend to be bears just waking up after a long winter of hibernation. Have them lie on their backs with their eyes open, keeping as still as possible. Choose someone to be "it." The child who is "it" should walk around and try to make the sleepy bears laugh by making funny faces but not touching them. Anyone who giggles is "out." The last bear left becomes the next "it."

Mitten Match

Bring in several pairs of mittens or gloves. Show all of the pairs before putting them into a large paper bag. Divide the class into two teams. Call on one child at a time to come to the bag and, without looking, pull out two items. If the two items are a matching pair, have the child place them beside the bag. Award that child's team one point. If the two items do not match, tell the child to put them back into the bag. After all of the pairs have been matched, count up each team's points to determine a winner.

Seasonal Charades

Have students act out scenes from seasonal activities. Use the suggestions listed below or come up with your own. Call on one child at a time to come to the front of the class. Whisper into her ear which activity you want her to act out. Ask other students to watch and guess what winter activity she is pretending to do.

Have students pretend to:

- build a snowman.
- ice skate.
- snow ski.
- put on winter clothes.
- shovel snow from a sidewalk.
- hibernate.
- migrate.
- catch snowflakes on their tongues.
- make snow angels.
- have a snowball fight.
- swim in the ocean.
- build a sand castle.
- put on sunscreen.
- be a butterfly.
- be a flower.
- be leaves falling from a tree.
- eat an ice-cream cone.

Baby Games

Tell children, "It is so much fun to remember all the fun you had when you were a baby. Babies play a lot of games and have a lot of people to play with. Can you remember some of the games that you played when you were a baby?"

The children may or may not remember. Remind them of the games "Patty Cake, Patty Cake," "Ring Around the Rosy," and "London Bridge Is Falling Down." The most mature four-year-old will still enjoy playing these games. Play any other games that the children are able to remember.

Hopping Races

Children naturally love to hop and jump. Add fine motor skills in with clothespins, tongs, and spoons. Use this natural energy by leading children in a variety of hopping races:

• Burlap sack race

• Three-legged race (Preschoolers are not very good at this race, but they sure have fun trying!)

• Egg on a spoon race

• Pick up a cotton ball with a clothespin race

• Big hopping/little hopping races

• Quiet, tiptoe hopping race (End the races with this one.)

Dinosaur Bone Drop

Materials: bag of clothespins (old-fashioned push style if possible), large coffee can or plastic fishbowl, white paint, paintbrush

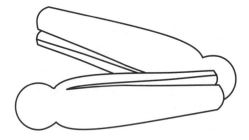

Children will create dinosaur movements and noises in this activity. Paint the clothespins white to represent dinosaur bones. Allow children to take turns standing over the coffee can or fishbowl and dropping the "dinosaur bones" into the target. Encourage them to improve their scores each time.

Ice Pass

Materials: small cooler with 5–7 small ice cubes

This is an especially fun cool-down activity after playing outside on a warm day. Talk about the properties of ice and the differences between solids and liquids. Have children stand up in a circle. Choose a leader to take an ice cube and show it to the group. Have him say the number "one" and then pass it to the person next to him. Tell children to continue passing the ice cube around the circle. Each time it goes through the leader's hands, the leader counts and says the next number. How many times will the ice travel around the circle before it melts? Would the number be different outside, on a hot day, or on a cold day? During the next round, have children try to think of ways to melt the ice faster or slower.

Dot-to-Dot Mural

Materials: butcher paper or craft paper roll, circles cut out of self-adhesive paper or paper with tape on back

Hang a length of paper on a wall at children's eye level. Give each child several self-stick dots. Let children place their circles all over the butcher paper. Take a moment to look at all of the dots. Then, have children use crayons to draw lines from dot to dot on the paper. As the children work to connect the dots, sing the following song:

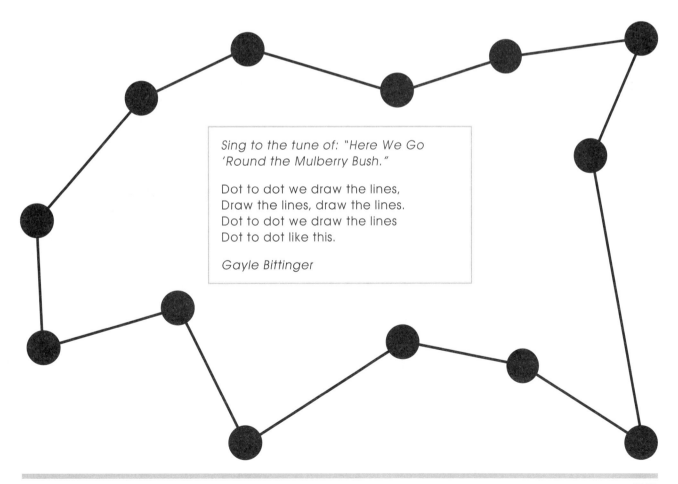

Sing to the tune of: "Here We Go 'Round the Mulberry Bush."

Dot to dot we draw the lines,
Draw the lines, draw the lines.
Dot to dot we draw the lines
Dot to dot like this.

Gayle Bittinger

Hand Harmonies

As they sit in a circle, encourage children to experiment with using their hands and bodies to produce musical sounds. Here are a few simple hand and body music ideas to teach them:

Hand Clapping: Have children clap the palms of their hands together in different ways. Have them try clapping with their palms stretched flat and with palms cupped.

Thigh Slapping: Have children slap their inner and outer thighs with their hands.

Cheek Clapping: Have children lightly slap their cheeks with their fingers, opening and closing their mouths to make different sounds.

Head Drum: Have children knock on various parts of their heads as a drum.

Full-Body Slap: Have children start at their head and work their way down their bodies, lightly slapping their front sides and their back sides with their palms or the pads of their fingers.

Finger Snapping: Teach children how to touch their thumbs and middle fingers together to snap. Have them press them together and then slide them quickly apart to make a snapping sound.

Moneybags: Fill children's pockets with coins and have them drum their hands against them.

Hand Rub: Have children rub their hands together at different speeds. (This also generates heat.)

Candy Roll: Show children how to rub a piece of cellophane or candy wrapper between their hands. (This will produce a nice crinkling sound.)

Partner Jive

Pair off the children. Have them face their partners and gently slap their hands together. Show them how to give each other a "high five" by slapping just one hand each together. Have children work together to make up their own musical routines combining partner slapping, high five, and Hand Harmonies techniques.

Musical Chairs and More

Materials: carpet squares, recorded music, chairs, index cards, large plastic hoops

Try these variations of the traditional Musical Chairs game with children. Everyone will enjoy the variety of games that can be played in a no-lose way.

Musical Carpet Squares: Arrange one carpet square for each child in a circle. Play some music and let children march around the squares. Stop the music and have each child find a carpet square to sit on. Repeat, leaving all of the carpet squares in place each time.

Musical Hugs: Play some music and ask everyone to dance around the room. When the music stops, have each child find another child (or two or three) to hug. Play the music again, stopping for hugs as you wish.

Musical Names: Arrange chairs in a circle, one for each child. Write each child's name on an index card and tape one card to each chair. Play some music and have children march around the chairs. When the music stops, have each child find the chair with her name on it. Then, switch the chairs around.

Musical Hoops: Collect several large plastic hoops (about one for every three or four children). Arrange the hoops on the floor in a circle. Play some music and have children walk around the hoops. When the music stops, have each child find a hoop to be in. (More than one child will be in each hoop.) Start the music and remove one hoop. Have children walk around the hoops until the music stops again and they must find a hoop to be in. Repeat until only one hoop is left. Stand back and watch the children's creativity and cooperation skills grow as they figure out a way for everyone to be inside the last hoop.

Make It Pop

Let children's imaginations make this activity sizzle. Tell children that they are all popcorn kernels sitting in a hot pan. Have them crouch down low and make sizzling noises. Then, have them pretend that they are getting hotter and hotter. What happens when they get really hot? Don't forget the sound effects! Also, sing the following song:

Popcorn Popping

Sing to the tune of: "Old MacDonald Had a Farm."

Popcorn popping, oh, what fun,
Popping big and white.
We will wait until it's done,
Then, we'll grab a bite.
With a pop, pop here
And a pop, pop there,
Here a pop, there a pop,
Everywhere a pop, pop.
Popcorn popping, oh, what fun,
Popping big and white.

Elizabeth McKinnon

Pancake Stretches

Talk about pancakes with children. What do they look and taste like? How are they served? Then, have children spread out on the floor and pretend to be pancakes. Should they lie on their backs or on their stomachs? If you wish, divide children into groups of three or more and let them come up with ways to safely stack parts of their bodies, such as hands, arms, and legs, on top of each other. Pretend to pour syrup on the stack and let children wiggle as it spreads all over them.

Fish in the Sea

Science, language development, and movement are integrated into this fun activity. Arrange children into two rows facing each other. Have children hold out their arms and each hold hands with the person facing her. Recite the poem "Jolly Fishermen" to the children. Ask one child at a time to name a fish or a sea creature (be ready to give suggestions). If a child chooses a shark, for example, have that child pretend to be a shark as he "swims" under everyone's arms. Incorporate the sea creature the child is pretending to be (a shark) into the second verse of the poem.

Jolly Fisherman

We are jolly fishermen.
Jolly fishermen are we.
Which sea creatures will we see today
As we sail upon the sea?
Shark, shark, shark,
We see a shark.
A shark swam near our boat today
As we sailed upon the sea.

Carol Gnojewski

London Bridge

This activity will help children explore their bodies' capacity for moving to music. Arrange children in two rows facing each other. Have the facing pairs hold their hands together and lift their arms up high to form a bridge. Then, have the first pair run under the bridge. When they get to the end of the bridge, have them hold hands and become part of the bridge again. Continue until children are familiar with the process of running under and re-forming the bridge. Then, sing the song "London Bridge." At the end of the first verse, have children lower their hands, trapping whomever is inside. Sing the second verse, moving hands from side to side. At the end of the verse, let the children go, and sing the song again. Continue while interest lasts.

London Bridge

London bridge is falling
down,
Falling down, falling down.

London bridge is falling
down,
My fair lady.

Shake the butter
side to side,
Side to side, side to side.

Shake the butter
side to side,
My fair lady.

Adapted Traditional

Sandwich Squish

Have children stand in a circle. Select one child to be peanut butter and one to be jelly. Have the two children stand in the middle of the circle. The children in the circle make up the bread. Together, sing "Hug Sandwich" and act out the movements indicated.

Hug Sandwich
Sing to the tune of: "I'm a Little Teapot."

I'm the peanut butter.
(First child points to self.)
I'm the jelly.
(Second child points to self.)
We stick together
Belly to belly.
(Children in the middle hug each other.)
Bread will gently squeeze us,
(Circle of children move forward and hug children in the middle.)
Squish, squish, squish.
We make a yummy
Hug sandwich!

Color Code Game

Have children take a good look at the clothes they are wearing for the day. What colors do they like wearing the best? Adapt the following song to incorporate the colors of the children's clothing. Vary the actions in the last line of the song. If you wish, direct children to do more than two actions. Make sure that every child participates at least once.

Where are the Colors?
Sing to the tune of: "Oh Where, Oh Where, Has My Little Dog Gone?"

Oh where, oh where are the kids with blue on?
Oh where, oh where could they be?
Oh where, oh where are the kids with blue on?
Twirl around for all to see.

Color Square Dance

Materials: green, yellow, blue, and red construction paper; hole punch; yarn

Learning how to square dance takes a lot of practice. Keep movements and directions clear and simple. Cut squares out of green, yellow, blue, and red construction paper. Punch a hole in the top of each square. Thread yarn through the holes to make a necklace for each child. Explain that in a square dance, one person is a "caller," who calls out the movements that everyone else performs. In a Color Square Dance, the caller instructs dancers to move by color, so children will need to know the color of their necklaces. Have children form a big circle and dance the "Do-Si-Do" according to the color directions you call out.

Do-Si-Do

Blues step forward
Then turn around.
Walk to your place
And twirl around.
Reds hop to the middle
And back again.
Find the yellows
And shake their hands.
Now greens, you slowly
Turn around.
Clap your hands
And make a sound.
Do-si-do,
Around we go,
All the colors
Step heel to toe.

Jean Warren

Bell Stories

Materials: small jingle bells

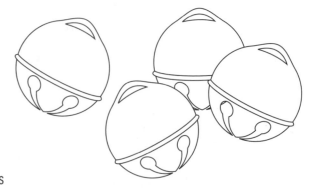

Adding a new element to story time will help young children practice their listening skills. Provide each child with a bell. Tell children a simple folk tale, such as "Goldilocks and the Three Bears" or "The Three Billy Goats Gruff." Designate one word, such as *Goldilocks* or *goat*, as a bell-ringing word. Have children listen carefully for that word and ring their bells whenever they hear you say it. To create a new version, make up a story about bells, such as a sleigh-riding story, a church bell story, or a fairy story. Have children ring their bells every time they hear the word *bell*.

Story Bell

Materials: small jingle bells

Promoting language development and self-expression is vital for preschool children. Sit in the middle of the circle with a small jingle bell. Begin a simple story related to the season, an upcoming holiday or event, or a theme that your class has been studying. Ring the bell to invite someone to take your place in the center of the circle and continue your story. Tell the child in the center to ring the bell when he or she wants to pass the story on to another storyteller. Gently remind each storyteller before she begins to keep her thoughts short so that others can take a turn.

106

Drumstick Hunt

Materials: drum, drumsticks or other classroom objects that will make sound

This activity engages children in exploring the element of sound. Drums are not always played by hand. Drumsticks, brushes, or mallets can also be used to produce different drumming sounds. Have children go on a drumstick hunt throughout the classroom in search of safe and interesting materials to use as drumsticks. Safe, impromptu drumsticks might include wooden dowels, craft sticks, action figures, paintbrushes, thimbles, unsharpened pencils, and measuring spoons. Invite each child to bring one drumstick to the circle. Pass a drum around the circle and give each child a turn to use what he found to use as a drumstick. If safety is in question, wrap tape or foam around the drumming ends of sticks, pencils, and dowels to make them safe for the children and the drum.

Name Chant

Materials: drum

Recognizing one's name and hearing it shared by others in a musical way is a positive experience for young children. Bring a drum to the circle and set it in front of you. Have each child say her name aloud. Spend time exploring each name by chanting it several times. Drum the name on the drum as you chant and count the number of beats. Accent the main syllable with a stronger drumbeat. Encourage children to listen and compare the different sounds that names make.

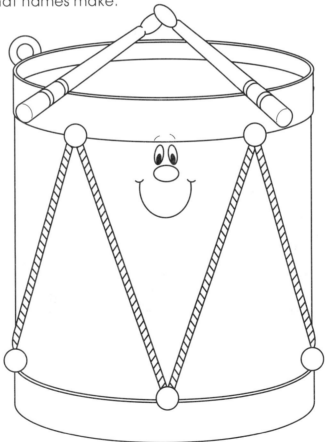

Drumbeat Movement

Materials: hand drum

Play a simple pattern on a hand drum that will encourage children to move their feet. Have children decide if this is a fast beat for running, a slow beat for walking, or perhaps a soft beat for tiptoeing. Then, let them show you. Stop drumming and have children freeze in place. Begin drumming a different pattern. Have children choose another way to move their feet. As they become familiar with this activity, switch drumming patterns without stopping. Challenge children to hear the differences and change their movements accordingly.

Streamer Fun

Materials: crepe paper, plastic lids, ribbon, cardboard tubes

Encourage children's creative movements by providing them with a variety of streamers, such as the ones described below. Let them use the streamers while dancing and moving to different kinds of music.

Simple Streamer: Cut 2-foot (0.6-m) lengths of crepe paper or ribbon. Put 10 strips together and staple them at one end to make a streamer.

Ring Streamer: Cut out the center of a plastic lid to make a ring. Staple two-foot (0.6-m) lengths of crepe paper or ribbon to one side of the ring. Leave the other side free for holding onto.

Tube Streamer: Staple two-foot (0.6-m) lengths of crepe paper or ribbon to the end of a long cardboard tube to make a tube streamer.

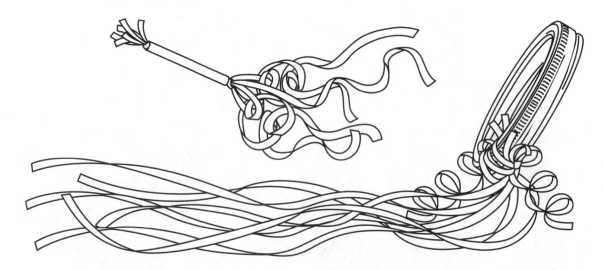

Rhythm Time

Materials: rhythm sticks, wooden blocks, triangles

The joy of music is central in the experiences teachers share with children. Give rhythm sticks and wooden blocks to some of the children and triangles to others. As you recite "Hickory, Dickory, Dock," have children with the sticks tap out the clock rhythm and those with triangles strike the hour.

Hickory, Dickory, Dock

Hickory, dickory, dock,
The mouse ran up the clock.
The clock struck one,
And down he did run.
Hickory, dickory, dock.

Traditional

Additional verses: The clock struck two, And down he flew; The clock struck three, And down he did flee; The clock struck four, He ran to the floor; The clock struck five, And he came alive.

Tap Math

Materials: number cards, rhythm sticks

Shuffle the deck of number cards. Have children sit in a circle and give them two rhythm sticks each. Sit in the middle of the circle as the card dealer. Take the card from the top of the deck and show it to children. What number is it? Ask children to say the number out loud. Then, have children tap out that number of beats with their sticks.

Continue while interest lasts. If you wish, let children take turns being the card dealer.

Name Clap

This activity is a good icebreaker at the beginning of the school year as children are learning names. Begin clapping in a slow rhythm. Invite children to begin clapping with you so that you are all clapping together in the same rhythm. Continue clapping as you go around the circle saying each child's name in rhythm. If you wish, add an extra challenge to this clapping game. While everyone continues to clap, say your name and then call out the name of someone else in the circle. That person will then repeat his name and call out the name of someone else. For example, you might say "Cait-lin, Bail-ey." Bailey would then say, "Bail-ey, Ty-e-sha." Tyesha would repeat her name and then call out to someone else.

Clapping Around

This activity gives children opportunities to incorporate movement and music. Have children pay attention and follow your lead as you clap and sing "Go Like This" below. Try clapping in funny places and positions, such as clapping near your ears, clapping over your head, clapping while bending your body forward, and clapping while twirling around. Invite the children to come up with other fun ways to clap.

> **Go Like This**
> *Sing to the tune of: "If You're Happy and You Know It."*
>
> If you're watching and you see me, go like this. (Clap, clap.)
> If you're watching and you see me, go like this. (Clap, clap.)
> If you're watching what I do,
> Then, you try to do it too.
> If you're watching and you see me, go like this. (Clap, clap.)
>
> *Heather Tekavec*

110

Listening for Pitch

Explain to children that when they listen for the "highness" or the "lowness" of a sound, they are listening for pitch. Gather them in a circle and have them listen as you play notes on a piano, a xylophone, a flute, or a recorder. Invite children to stretch up high as a tree or a giraffe's neck when they hear high notes and curl up low as a snake, a seed, or a ball when they hear low notes.

Volume Up, Volume Down

Volume of music is an important element for young children to understand. Teach children a simple song such as "Mary Had a Little Lamb" or "Three Blind Mice." Have them sing it softly first, then at medium volume, then loudly. How did the different volumes change the song? Which volume did they like best? Next, talk about the dynamics of everyday sounds. Have children come up with examples of sounds that are soft, medium, or loud. Would a mouse's squeak be soft or loud? What about a lion's roar? Or, a dripping faucet or a honking car? Accept all logical suggestions and answers.

Introduce new vocabulary by explaining that composers indicate dynamics, or how loudly or softly music should be played, using words such as *piano* (soft), *mezzo* (medium), and *forte* (loud).

Music Detectives

Using auditory discrimination clues, children will enjoy being "music detectives." Have children sit in a circle in the middle of the room with their eyes closed. (Provide them with blindfolds to pull over their eyes to keep them from peeking if you wish.) Move around the circle, humming or singing a simple tune. Invite children to listen carefully and try to figure out where they think the music is coming from. Stay in one spot and have children point to where they think the music is. Then, have them open their eyes (or remove their blindfolds). Did they guess correctly? Let children take turns being the music detectives and the singer.

Musical Echoes

Simple rhymes and chants engage children's love for repetition and predictability. Invite children to form a circle with you in the middle. Make sure that all of the children are facing you. Then, choose a simple, general theme, such as fruits, animals, flowers, or toys. Chant, "I like _____," and complete the sentence with a specific example of the theme you have chosen, such as "I like peaches" or "I like dogs." Have children repeat your sentence back to you. Give each child a turn in the middle.

Have each child build upon your sentence, so "I like peaches" becomes "I like peaches and plums" and then "I like peaches, plums, and cherries."

Froggy Freeze

Materials: colored tape, music

In a wide open space teach children how to hop like a frog, crouching down and then springing forward. Place several (at least one per child) tape *X*'s on the floor and ask each "frog" to hop to one. When the music starts, the "frogs" will hop around the floor. When the music stops, yell out "Froggy Freeze!" and each "frog" is to hop to an *X* and freeze until the music starts again.

Percussion Instruments

Materials: recycled materials

Children enjoy playing "orchestra" to the rhythm of a musical selection. Tapping, clapping together, striking, shaking, or beating instruments, when done lightly and in rhythm, produces a pleasant effect as an accompaniment to music. The performance also gives great satisfaction to the children.

You can make many interesting percussion instruments out of everyday objects. Here are some suggestions:

Jack and Jill Shakers: tubes from rolls of paper towels with ends sealed and beads inside (You may even cover the tubes with decorative paper.)

Rattle Caps: bottle caps strung on a wire ring or a coat hanger

Clatter Cups: two paper cups sealed together with tape and about three marbles inside

Ridged Block: a board with ridges sawed across it; play by scraping with a pencil or a thin stick.

Clickety Clothespins: 8 or 10 upside-down clothespins nailed or screwed to a thin board from the underside; play with a rhythm stick or a wooden craft stick.

Paper Tambourine: two paper plates sewed or tied together and with bells tied on

Dribble Drum: 1-pound (0.45-kg) coffee can one-third full of water, inner tube stretched over top and tied on tightly or sealed with heavy rubber binders

Marching Band Parade

Materials: several of each of the following kinds of rhythm instruments: drums, tambourines, bells, triangles, rhythm sticks, sand blocks, etc.; basket or box

Children will identify rhythm instruments and move to the rhythm of the music they play. Place instruments in a basket or a box. Show children one instrument at a time and have them tell you the name of each instrument. Let them listen to the sounds each instrument makes. Point out the different materials that the instruments are made of and discuss their shapes and textures.

Give each child an instrument. Ask him how it is used. Let children explore the shapes, the textures, and the sounds of the instruments. Then, have children put their instruments down. Choose one group of children with the same instrument to play a soft rhythm beat. Let that group put their instruments down. Select another group of children with like instruments. Continue this process until all groups of instruments have been played.

Have children pick up their instruments and line up for a marching band parade. Encourage children to march together around the playground while playing their instruments. Then, go back to the classroom and discuss the marching band parade.

Six Little Ducks

Materials: copy of the song "Six Little Ducks" (page 115), CD player, CD of "Six Little Ducks," flannel board or magnetic whiteboard, yellow and orange felt squares, duck patterns (page 116)

Children will enjoy singing and moving to the classic song "Six Little Ducks." Using the patterns, cut out six felt ducks and the number six. Ask children what sounds a duck makes. Tell them that they are going to learn the song "Six Little Ducks." Before teaching them the song, let them meet the six little ducks. Bring each duck out one at a time and introduce it. Discuss the ducks' names (below) and why they might have been given that name.

Duck Names

1. *Shy* because she is afraid to talk to other ducks.
2. *Happy* because he is always happy and having fun.
3. *Tiny* because she is the smallest duck.
4. *Slow* because he is the slowest duck.
5. *Loud* because he is the loudest duck.
6. *Artsy* because she loves to paint.

Have children count the ducks. Place the number six on the felt board for children to see.

Have children practice walking like ducks. Encourage them to squat and flap their arms while they move about the room quacking.

Next, sing the song and/or play the song as children move about the room singing "Six Little Ducks."

Encourage children to sit in a circle and discuss which of the six ducks they are most like.

Six Little Ducks

Six little ducks that I once knew,
Fat ones, skinny ones, fair ones too.
But, the one little duck with the feather on his back
He led the others with his quack, quack, quack.
Quack, quack, quack—quack, quack, quack,
He led the others with his quack, quack, quack.

Down to the river they would go,
Wibble wobble, wibble wobble, to and fro.
But, the one little duck with the feather on his back
He led the others with his quack, quack, quack.
Quack, quack, quack—quack, quack, quack,
He led the others with his quack, quack, quack.

Home from the river they would come,
Wibble wobble, wibble wobble, ho-hum-hum.
But, the one little duck with the feather on his back
He led the others with his quack, quack, quack.
Quack, quack, quack—quack, quack, quack,
He led the others with his quack, quack, quack.

Six little ducks that I once knew,
Fat ones, skinny ones, fair ones too.
But, the one little duck with the feather on his back
He led the others with his quack, quack, quack.
Quack, quack, quack—quack, quack, quack,
He led the others with his quack, quack, quack.

Duck Patterns

All About Me

Traditional Songs

"If You're Happy and You Know It"
"The More We Get Together"
"Head, Shoulders, Knees and Toes"
"The Hokey Pokey"
"Looby Loo"
"Punchinello"
"Mary Wore Her Red Dress"
"Put Your Fingers in the Air"
"Where is Thumbkin?"

Adapted Songs

Isabelle Is Here Today

Sing to the tune of: "Farmer in the Dell."

Isabelle* is here today,
We're so happy, yes we are.
Isabelle is here today.
Isabelle is here today.

   * Sing each child's name in turn. Invite the
   child to jump or dance in the circle while
   it is her turn. You may finish with, "The boys
   are here today . . . ," "The girls are here
   today . . . ," and "Everyone is here today
   . . . ," and allow the appropriate children to
   jump or dance.

We Are Growing

Sing to the tune of: "Where Is Thumbkin?"

We are growing, we are changing,
Everyday, everyday.
All of us are different, but each of us is special
In our own way, in our own way.

Movement Activities

Music Interpretation

Play short excerpts of a variety of music types for children.
Allow them to move any way they wish to express their
feelings about the different types of music.

My Space

Talk with children about the need for personal space.
Have children bring in towels from home or use nap mats
and allow them to sit and play in their own spaces on the
towels or mats.

Apples

Adapted Songs

Little Apples
Sing to the tune of: "Ten Little Indians."

One little, two little, three little apples,
Four little, five little, six little apples,
Seven little, eight little, nine little apples,
On my apple tree.
Munch little, munch little, munch little apples,
Crunch little, crunch little, crunch little apples,
A bunch of little, bunch of little, bunch of little
   apples,
Good for you and me.

I'm a Little Squirrel
Sing to the tune of: "I'm a Little Teapot."

I'm a little squirrel, fuzzy and gray.
When autumn comes, I gather nuts all day,
So that when the winter comes, you see,
I'll have food for my family and me.

Leaves, Leaves Everywhere
Sing to the tune of: "Row, Row, Row Your Boat."

Leaves, leaves everywhere,
Falling off the trees,
Red and yellow, orange and brown,
A wonderful sight to see.

Apple, Apple on the Tree
Sing to the tune of: "Twinkle, Twinkle Little Star."

Apple, apple on the tree,
I know you are good for me.
You are fun to munch and crunch,
For a snack or in my lunch.
Apple, apple on the tree,
I know you are good for me.

Finger Play

The Apple Tree

Way up high in the apple tree, (Point up; then, hold arms in a circle overhead.)
Two little apples smiled at me. (Hold up two fingers; then, point to cheeks and smile.)
I shook that tree as hard as I could. (Pretend to shake a tree.)
Down came the apples. Mmm, they were good! (Point down; then, rub tummy.)

Farm Animals

Traditional Songs

"Old MacDonald"
"B-I-N-G-O"
"Five Little Ducks"
"Baa, Baa, Black Sheep"
"Mary Had a Little Lamb"

Adapted Songs

Can You . . . ?

Sing to the tune of: "Do Your Ears Hang Low?"

Can you *baa* like a sheep?
Can you *moo* like a cow?
Can you *neigh* like a horse?
Can you *quack* like a duck?
Can you *cluck* like a hen
Who is pecking in her pen?
Can you make that sound?

Milk, Milk, Milk the Cow

Sing to the tune of: "Row, Row, Row Your Boat."

Milk, milk, milk the cow,
While sitting on a stool,
Pulling, squirting,
Pulling, squirting,
Until the bucket's full.

Finger Plays

This Little Cow

This little cow eats grass, (Point to thumb.)
This little cow eats hay, (Point to index finger.)
This little cow drinks water, (Point to middle finger.)
This little cow runs away. (Point to ring finger.)
This little cow does nothing (Point to pinky.)
But sleep in the sun all day! (Place hands under head like a pillow.)

Two Mother Chickens

Two mother chickens lived in a pen.
    (Show thumbs.)
Each had four babies, and that made ten.
    (Show 10 fingers.)
These four babies were black as night,
    (Hold up four fingers on one hand.)
These four babies were fluffy and white.
    (Hold up four fingers on other hand.)
But, all eight babies loved to play,
And they pecked and pecked in the pen all day.
    (Bob head.)
At night, with their mothers, they curled up in a
    heap (Make fists, palms up.)
And chirped and chirped until they went to
    sleep.

Ocean

Traditional Songs

"Once I Caught a Fish Alive"
"Over in the Meadow in an Itty Bitty Pond"
"My Bonny Lies over the Ocean"

Adapted Songs

A-Fishing We Will Go
Sing to the tune of: "The Farmer in the Dell."

A-fishing we will go, a-fishing we will go,
We'll have some fun playing in the sun,
A-fishing we will go.

A-fishing we will go, a-fishing we will go,
Oh, how I wish to catch a fish,
A-fishing we will go.

When the Fish Go Swimming By
Sing to the tune of: "When the Saints Go Marching In."

Oh, when the fish go swimming by,
Oh, when the fish go swimming by,
I'll be on the shore watching closely,
When the fish go swimming by.

(Repeat, replacing *fish* with other ocean animal names.)

Finger Plays

Five Little Fish

Five little fish swimming in a school.   (Hold up five fingers; then, swim with hands.)
The first one said, "This water's cool."   (Hold up one finger; then, shiver.)
The second one said, "There's a shark over there!"   (Hold up two fingers; then, point excitedly.)
The third one said, "We'd better beware."   (Hold up three fingers; then, look scared.)
The fourth one said, "Where can we hide?"   (Hold up four fingers; then, hold out hands with shoulders shrugged.)

The fifth one said, "There's a cave! Go inside."   (Hold up five fingers; then, point.)
Then, in went the fish, and the shark went away,
And the five little fish swam out to play.

Eight Little Tentacles
Sing to the tune of: "Ten Little Indians."

One little, two little, three little tentacles,
Four little, five little, six little tentacles,
Seven little, eight, yes, eight little tentacles,
On an octopus.
(Have children hold up the correct number of fingers as they recite the finger play.)

Woodland Animals

Traditional Songs

"The Bear Went over the Mountain"
"Do Re Mi"
"Five Green and Speckled Frogs"
"Five Little Ducks"
"Hickory Dickory Dock"

"In a Cabin in the Wood"
"Little Bunny Foo Foo"
"Two Little Blackbirds"
"Over in the Meadow"
"There Once Was a Green Little Frog"

Adapted Song

I'm a Little Gopher
Sing to the tune of: "I'm a Little Teapot."

I'm a little gopher, furry and brown.
I play in the sun and sleep underground.
Sometimes, you will see me playing outside,
But when I'm scared, in my burrow I hide.

Finger Plays

The Wise Old Owl (Traditional)

A wise old owl sat in an oak.	(Make a fist and set on other forearm.)
The more he heard, the less he spoke.	(Cup hand around ear; then, cover lips.)
The less he spoke, the more he heard.	(Cover lips; then, cup hand around ear.)
Why aren't we all like that wise old bird?	(Hold out hands questioningly.)

My Turtle (Traditional)

This is my turtle.	(Make a fist with thumb extended.)
He lives in a shell.	(Tuck thumb inside fist.)
He likes his home very well.	
He pokes his head out	
When he wants to eat	(Extend thumb from fist.)
And pulls it back again	
When he wants to sleep.	(Tuck thumb inside fist.)

Winter

Adapted Songs

Hooray for Winter!
Sing to the tune of: "London Bridge."

Autumn has ended, winter is here, winter is here, winter is here.
Autumn has ended, winter is here.
Hooray for winter!
Other verses:
Get your coats and mittens too . . .
Bundle up, the weather is cold . . .
Snowy days, we want them soon . . .
Let's drink hot cocoa to warm us up . . .

Movement Activities

Snowman Dance

Play classical music and let children dance like falling snow. Then, have them "grow" into snowmen. After a few moments of standing like snowmen, have the students slowly "melt" to the ground.

Migration Formation

Share information about how geese fly in a *V* formation when migrating to warmer climates. Take children outside to a large open area. Organize them in a *V* formation. Tell the child at the point of the *V* that he will be leading the other "geese" south. Tell children that you will give a signal when the leader should move to the back of the flock, and a new leader should take over. Have children *honk* (or give them party horns) to encourage the other geese to stay in formation.

Finger Play

Bundle Up

Zip up your coat; put a hat on your head.
(Pretend to zip up coat and put on a hat.)
Pull on your boots if you want to sled!
(Pretend to put snow boots on.)
Mittens on hands, wrap your scarf on tight.
(Pretend to put mittens on and wrap a scarf around neck.)
Better bundle up or the snow will bite!
(Hug self and then snap hands together like alligator jaws.)

Transportation

Traditional Song

The Wheels on the Bus

The wheels on the bus go round and round,
Round and round, round and round.
The wheels on the bus go round and round,
All through the town.

Other bus verses:
People . . . go up and down; wipers . . . go *swish, swish, swish*; money . . . goes *clink, clink, clink*; mommies . . . say, "*Shh, shh, shh!*"; babies . . . cry, "*Waa, waa, waa!*"; driver . . . says, "Move on back"; doors . . . go open and shut; horn . . . goes *beep, beep, beep*.

Additional adapted verses to sing to the tune of "The Wheels on the Bus":

The wheels on the train go *clickety clack*,
Clickety clack, *clickety clack*.
The wheels on the train go *clickety clack*,
All along the track.

Additional train verses:
Whistle . . . goes *whoo, whoo, whoo!*; conductor . . . says, "All aboard!"; people . . . go bumpety bump;
brakes . . . go *chhhh, chhhh, chhhh*

The anchor on the ship goes up and down,
Up and down, up and down.
The anchor on the ship goes up and down
    Across the big blue ocean.

Additional ship verses:
People . . . have lots of fun; captain . . . says, "Full steam ahead!"; engine . . . goes *Rrrr!, Rrrr!, Rrrr!*

Other Traditional Songs

"Anchors Aweigh"
"Bumpin' Up and Down in My Little Red Wagon"
"Down by the Station"
"I've Been Working on the Railroad"
"Old Brass Wagon"
"Sailing, Sailing"
"Tinga Layo"

"Bicycle Built for Two"
"Camptown Ladies"
"I Love to Go A-Wandering"
"Off We Go into the Wild Blue Yonder"
"Row, Row, Row Your Boat"
"Three Jolly Fishermen"

Traditional Finger Plays

"Hurry, Hurry, Drive the Fire Truck"
"She'll be Comin' 'Round the Mountain"
"Skip to My Lou"

Related Nursery Rhymes

"The Noble Duke of York"
"Rub-a-Dub-Dub"
"This Is the Way a Lady Rides"

Dinosaurs

Adapted Songs

The Dinosaur Song
Sing to the tune of: "The Wheels on the Bus."

The *Tyrannosaurus rex* had great big teeth,
Great big teeth, great big teeth.
The *Tyrannosaurus rex* had great big teeth,
When the dinosaurs roamed.

Additional verses:
The *Apatosaurus* had a very long tail . . .
The *Diplodocus's* nostrils were on top of his head
   . . .
The *Saltopus* was as small as a cat . . .

Dinosaurs, Dinosaurs
Sing to the tune of: "Teddy Bear, Teddy Bear."

Dinosaurs, dinosaurs stomped around.
Dinosaurs, dinosaurs shook the ground.
Dinosaurs, dinosaurs far and near.
Dinosaurs, dinosaurs are no longer here.

The Dinosaurs Go Marching
Sing to the tune of: "The Ants Go Marching."

The dinosaurs go marching one by one, hurrah, hurrah.
The dinosaurs go marching one by one, hurrah, hurrah.
The dinosaurs go marching one by one, the little one
Stops to stand in the sun,
And they all go marching round and round and up and down.

Additional verses: Two . . . to admire the view
Three . . . to eat from a tree   Four . . . to give a roar
Five . . . to stay alive   Six . . . to gather some sticks
Seven . . . to count to eleven   Eight . . . to roller-skate.
Nine . . . to scratch his spine   Ten . . . to feel the wind

Dinosaur Activities

Dinosaur Stomping
Explain to children that some dinosaurs moved slowly and some moved quickly. Have children match your stomping rhythm. Then, have them match your stomping patterns, such as slow, slow, fast, fast, fast.

Which Dinosaur Are You?
Gather children and have them stand in a circle holding hands. Teach them the song that follows and then have them sing it while walking in a circle. At the end of the song, describe a dinosaur and have children guess which one you are describing. Sing to the tune of "Skip to My Lou": Who, who, who are you? Who, who, who are you? Who, who, who are you? Which dinosaur are you?

Nutrition

Adapted Songs

We're Going to the Grocery Store

Sing to the tune of: "Mary Had a Little Lamb."

We're going to the grocery store,
Grocery store, grocery store.
We'll buy our favorite food there,
(Child's name), what will you buy?
(Allow each child a turn to name a food.)

Ten Bottles of Milk in the Fridge

Sing to the tune of: "Ninety-Nine Bottles of Pop on the Wall."

Ten bottles of milk in the fridge,
Ten bottles of milk.
Take one out and drink it all up,
Nine bottles of milk in the fridge.
(Continue singing and counting backward to one.)

Finger Plays

Two Little Apples

Way up high on the apple tree,
    (Point as if pointing to top of a tree.)
Two little apples smiled at me.
    (Hold up two fingers; then, point to smile.)
I shook that tree as hard as I could,
    (Pretend to shake tree.)
Down came the apples. Mmm, mmm, good!
    (Rub tummy.)

Five Shiny Oranges

Five shiny oranges hanging in a tree,
    (Hold up five fingers.)
The juiciest oranges you ever did see.
    (Point to your eyes.)
The wind came by and gave an angry frown,
    (Make a frown face.)
And one shiny orange came tumbling down.
    (Hold up one finger; then, roll hands.)

Related Nursery Rhymes

"Georgie Porgie"   "Hot Cross Buns"   "Humpty Dumpty"
"I'm a Little Teapot"   "Jack Sprat"   "Little Jack Horner"
"Little Miss Muffet"   "Little Tommy Tucker"   "Patty Cake"
"Pease Porridge Hot"   "Peter Piper"   "Polly Put the Kettle On"
"The Queen of Hearts"   "Simple Simon"   "Sing a Song of Sixpence"
"This Little Piggy Went to Market"   "To Market, To Market"

Traditional Rhymes

The Candy Store

I met some friends at the candy store.
We bought candy,
We bought cake,
We went home with a bellyache.
Mama, Mama, we feel sick.
Call the doctor, quick, quick, quick!
Doctor, doctor, will we live?
Close your eyes and count to five.
One, two, three, four, five.
Hooray, we're alive!

The Grapefruit

I wish I were a grapefruit,
And here's the reason why:
When you come to eat me,
I'll squirt you in the eye!

All About Me

Children love finger plays and listening to the rhymes in poetry. Begin the school year with one of the finger plays and gradually add the others. Spend time on finger plays daily. Children enjoy the repetition and the feelings of mastery.

Who Feels Happy Today?

Who feels happy at school today?
All who do, snap your fingers this way.
Who feels happy at school today?
All who do, clap your hands this way.
Who feels happy at school today?
All who do, wink your eye this way.
Who feels happy at school today?
All who do, fold your hands this way.

(Ask children, "What makes you feel happy? Can you show a motion you like to do when you are happy?")

What I Can Do

I can spin just like a top.
Look at me! Look at me!
I have feet and I can hop.
Look at me! Look at me!
I have hands and I can clap.
Look at me! Look at me!
I can lay them in my lap.
Look at me! Look at me!

(Have children act out this rhyme. Ask them, "What else can your feet do? What else can your hands do?")

I Am Special

Sing to the tune of: "Where Is Thumbkin?"

I am special. (Point to self.)
I am special. (Point to self.)
If you look, (Put hand above eyes.)
You will see, (Point to eyes.)
Someone very special, (Nod head yes.)
Someone very special, (Nod head yes.)
Yes, it's me! (Point to self confidently.)
Yes, it's me! (Point to self confidently.)

(This is a good poem to use to develop a positive self-image and feelings of self-worth.)

I Am in Between

Giraffes are tall,
    (Hold hands high.)
Monkeys are small,
    (Hold hands low.)
And zebras are in between.
    (Hold hands at waist level.)
Adults are tall,
    (Stand on tiptoe.)
Babies are small,
    (Crouch low.)
And I am in between!
    (Stand; then, point to self.)

Wiggles

A wiggle, wiggle here,   Wiggle your knees,
A wiggle, wiggle there.   And move your lips.
Wiggle your hands,   Wiggle, wiggle, wiggle,
Up in the air.   And wiggle and bend.
Wiggle your shoulders,   Wiggle, wiggle, wiggle,
Wiggle your hips,   And this is the end!

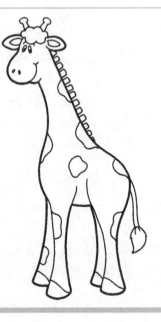

All About Me

When I Was One

When I was one, I was so small,	(Hold up one finger.)
I could not speak a word at all.	(Shake head.)
When I was two, I learned to walk.	(Hold up two fingers.)
I learned to sing, I learned to walk.	(Walk in place.)
When I was three, I grew and grew.	(Hold up three fingers.)
Now I am four, and so are you!	(Hold up four fingers; then, point to another person.)

Five Fingers on Each Hand

I have five fingers on each hand,	(Hold up fingers of both hands.)
Ten toes on my two feet.	(Point to toes.)
Two ears, two eyes,	(Point to ears and then eyes.)
One nose, one mouth,	(Point to nose and then mouth.)
With which to gently speak.	(Continue pointing to mouth.)
My hands can clap, my feet can tap,	(Clap hands; then, tap feet.)
My eyes can brightly shine.	(Point to eyes.)
My ears can hear,	(Cup hands behind ears.)
My nose can sniff,	(Wiggle nose.)
My mouth can speak a rhyme.	(Point to mouth.)

Hands on Hips

Hands on hips; now, turn around.
Plant your feet here in the ground.
Twist your hips; now, stretch and bend.
Turn around and smile at a friend.
Bend your body, sway and sway.
That is all we'll do today!

(Read very slowly so that children will have
sufficient time to perform each action.)

All About Me

Here are my ears, and here is my nose.
Here are my fingers, and here are my toes.
Here are my eyes, both open wide.
Here is my mouth with my teeth inside
And my busy tongue that helps me speak.
Here is my chin, and here are my cheeks.
Here are my hands that help me play
And my feet that run about all day.

(Touch each body part when mentioned.)

All About Me

One, Two, Three

One, two, three.
One, two, three.
How many children
Make one, two, three?
_____ and _____ and _____ make three.
Please come and stand in front of me.

(Use the names of children in the class in the blanks. After three children respond, call on another three until all of the children have had a turn. This poem can also serve as an experience for roll call.)

Two Little Houses

Two little houses closed up tight.   (Show two closed fists.)
Open the window and let in the light.   (Spread hands apart.)
Ten little people tall and straight.   (Hold up ten fingers.)
Ready for school at half past eight.   (Make running motion with fingers)

Friends

I have two friends,   (Hold up two fingers on left hand.)
And they have me.   (Hold up one finger on right hand.)
Two friends and me,   (Bend each finger from left to right.)
That's one, two, three.   (Hold up fingers while saying "1,2,3.")

That's Me, Complete!

I have ten little fingers and ten little toes,   (Hold up 10 fingers.)
Two little arms and one little nose,   (Raise arms.)
One little mouth and two little ears,   (Point to mouth and ears.)
Two little eyes for smiles and tears,   (Smile.)
One little head and two little feet,   (Shake head.)
One little chin, that's ME, complete!   (Hold arms up.)

Color Rhyme

If your clothes have any red,
(Do actions as rhyme indicates.)
Put your finger on your head.

If your clothes have any blue,
Put your finger on your shoe.

If your clothes have any green,
Wave your hand so that you're seen.

If your clothes have any yellow,
Smile like a happy fellow.

If your clothes have any brown,
Turn your smile into a frown.

If your clothes have any black,
Put your hands behind your back.

If your clothes have any white,
Stamp your feet with all your might!

All About Me

Silly Face

Silly face, silly face, what do you see?
I see a sleepy face looking at me!
Sleepy face, sleepy face, what do you see?
I see an angry face looking at me!
Angry face, angry face, what do you see?
I see a surprised face looking at me!
Surprised face, surprised face, what do you see?
I see a sad face looking at me!
Sad face, sad face, what do you see?
I see a happy face looking at me!
Happy face, happy face, what do you see?
I see another happy face looking at me!

(Turn this rhyme into a group activity. Display pictures of silly, sleepy, angry, surprised, sad, and happy faces. Have children make these facial expressions.)

A Japanese Game

Hana, hana, hana, kuchi;
Kuchi, kuchi, kuchi, mimi;
Mimi, mimi, mimi, me.

Nose, nose, nose, mouth;
Mouth, mouth, mouth, ear;
Ear, ear, ear, eye.

Traditional

Fun with Hands

Roll, roll, roll your hands,
As slow as slow can be.
Roll, roll, roll your hands,
Do it now with me.
Roll, roll, roll your hands,
As fast as fast can be.
Roll, roll, roll your hands,
Do it now with me.

(Continue this action rhyme by substituting these phrases: Clap, clap, clap your hands;
Shake, shake, shake your hands;
Stamp, stamp, stamp your feet.)

I Wiggle

I wiggle my fingers.
I wiggle my toes.
I wiggle my shoulders.
I wiggle my nose.
Now, no more wiggles are left in me.
So, I will sit still as still can be.

(Follow directions in verse.)

Two Little Feet Go Tap

Two little feet go tap, tap, tap.   (Tap feet.)
Two little hands go clap, clap, clap.   (Clap hands.)
A quick little leap up from my chair,   (Stand quickly.)
Two little arms reach high in the air.   (Stretch arms high.)

Two little feet go jump, jump, jump.   (Jump.)
Two little fists go thump, thump, thump.   (Pound fists.)
One little body goes round and round,   (Twirl around.)
And one little child sits quietly down.   (Sit.)

Counting

Ten Huge Dinosaurs

Ten huge dinosaurs were standing in a line.
One tripped on a cobblestone, and then there were nine.

Nine huge dinosaurs were trying hard to skate.
One cracked right through the ice, and then there were eight.

Eight huge dinosaurs were counting past eleven.
One counted up too far, and then there were seven.

Seven huge dinosaurs learned some magic tricks.
One did a disappearing act, and then there were six.

Six huge dinosaurs were learning how to drive.
One forgot to put in gas, and then there were five.

Five huge dinosaurs joined the drum corps.
One forgot the drumsticks, and then there were four.

Four huge dinosaurs were wading in the sea.
One waded too far out, and then there were three.

Three huge dinosaurs looked for Mister Soo.
One gave up the search, and then there were two.

Two huge dinosaurs went to the Amazon.
One sailed in up to his head, and then there was one.

One lonesome dinosaur knew her friends had gone.
She found a big museum, and then there were none.

(Make "ten huge dinosaurs." Use on a flannel board or as stick puppets.)

One, Two, How Do You Do?

1, 2, how do you do?
1, 2, 3, clap with me;
1, 2, 3, 4, jump on the floor;
1, 2, 3, 4, 5, let's look happy and alive.

(This is a good action poem to use before getting children in line for outdoor play. Or, use it to help children "let off steam" on a rainy day.)

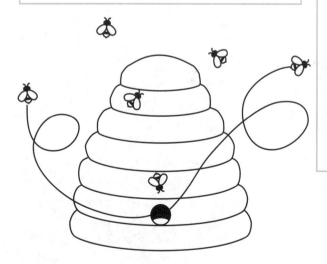

Six Buzzing Bumblebees

Six buzzing bumblebees flying 'round the hive,
    (Hold up six fingers.)
One buzzes off, and that leaves five.
    (Hold up five fingers of one hand.)
Five buzzing bumblebees flying near my door,
One buzzes off, and that leaves four.
    (Bend down thumb.)
Four buzzing bumblebees flying 'round a tree,
One buzzes off, and that leaves three.
    (Bend down index finger.)
Three buzzing bumblebees in the sky so blue,
One buzzes off, and that leaves two.
    (Bend down middle finger.)
Two buzzing bumblebees flying by the sun,
One buzzes off, and that leaves one.
    (Bend down ring finger.)
One buzzing bumblebee looking for some fun,
It buzzes off, and that leaves none.
    (Bend down little finger.)

Counting

Five Little Bunnies

Five little bunnies hopping all around.
The first bunny said, "I'm going to town."
The second bunny said, "I'll hide the eggs."
The third bunny said, "I will stretch my legs."
The fourth bunny said, "I'll eat a carrot."
The fifth bunny said, "I'll scare a parrot."
Five little bunnies, so soft and furry,
Ran around the yard in such a hurry.

Five Shiny Oranges

Five shiny oranges hanging in a tree.
   (Hold up five fingers.)
The juiciest oranges you ever did see.
   (Point to your eyes.)
The wind came by—whoosh was the sound,
   (Wave hands.)
And one shiny orange came tumbling down.
   (Hold up one finger; then, roll hands.)

Three Little Penguins

Three little penguins dressed in white and black,
Waddle, waddle forward and waddle right back.
Three little penguins, in a funny pose.
They are wearing their evening clothes.
Their suits are black and their vests are white.
They waddle to the left and they waddle to the right.
They stand on the ice and they look very neat,
As they waddle along on their little flat feet.

(Ask: "Where might we see penguins? Where have you seen one? How are penguins different from other birds?" Have children act out this rhyme. Then, ask them to draw penguins.)

Five Little Ducks

Five little ducks swimming on the lake.

The first one said, "Watch the waves I make."

The second duck said, "Swimming is such fun."

The third duck said, "I would rather sit in the sun."

The fourth duck said, "Let's swim away."

The fifth duck said, "Oh, let's stay."

Then, along came a motorboat with a pop, pop, pop, (Clap hands together three times.)

And the five little ducks swam away from the spot.

Ten Giants

Not last night	(Shake head "no.")
But the night before,	
Ten giants	(Hold up all 10 fingers.)
Broke down my door!	
As I ran out,	(Make fingers "run out.")
They came in,	(Make fingers "run in.")
Put on some music,	(Spin around.)
And began to spin!	
1-2-3-4-5-6-7-8-9-10	

Counting

Six Little Ducks

Six little ducks went out to play, over the hill and far away.
When the mother duck went "Quack, quack, quack,"
Five little ducks came waddling back.
Five little ducks went out to play, over the hill and far away.
When the mother duck went "Quack, quack, quack,"
Four little ducks came waddling back.
Four little ducks went out to play, over the hill and far away.
When the mother duck went "Quack, quack, quack,"
Three little ducks came waddling back.
Three little ducks went out to play, over the hill and far away.
When the mother duck went "Quack, quack, quack,"
Two little ducks came waddling back.
One little duck went out to play, over the hill and far away.
When the mother duck went "Quack, quack, quack,"
One little duck came waddling back.
When the mother duck went "Quack, quack, quack,"
All the little ducks came home.

Five Little Koalas

Five little koalas in a eucalyptus tree.
The first one said, "Hey, look at me!"
The second one said, "I have pretty furry hair."
The third one said, "I don't have a care."
The fourth one said, "Australia is my home."
The fifth one said, "I'll never, ever roam!"
Five little koalas in a eucalyptus tree,
Climbing and playing and happy to be free!

Five Fat Walruses

Five fat walruses were at the North Pole.   (Hold up five fingers.)
One climbed upon the ice and fell into a hole.
Four fat walruses swam toward the ice.   (Hold up four fingers.)
One bumped an iceberg, which wasn't very nice.
Three fat walruses had whiskers on their faces.   (Hold up three fingers.)
One got bored and went to sleep; he didn't like the places.
Two fat walruses went to look for food.   (Hold up two fingers.)
One swam far, far away; he wasn't in the mood.
One fat walrus was tired of the play.   (Hold up one finger.)
She flipped a good-bye with her tail and then she swam away.

Two Little Apples

Way up high on the apple tree,
(Point as if pointing to the top of a tree.)

Two little apples smiled at me.
(Hold up two fingers; then, point to smile.)

I shook that tree as hard as I could.
(Pretend to shake tree.)

Down came the apples. Mmm, mmm, good!
(Rub tummy.)

Autumn

Autumn winds begin to blow;
(Blow.)
Colored leaves fall fast and slow.
(Make fast and slow falling motions with hands.)
Twirling, whirling all around.
(Turn self around and around.)
Until at last, they touch the ground.
(Fall to ground.)

Raking Leaves

I rake the leaves,   (Make raking motion.)
When they fall down,   (Raise arms and let fingers fall gradually.)
In a great big pile.   (Measure.)
And when there are
Enough of them,
I jump on them a while.   (Jump three times.)

Autumn Leaves

Leaves are floating softly down;   (Make "floating down" movements with hands.)
Some are red and some are brown.
The wind goes swish through the air;   (Make "swish" motion with one hand.)
When you look back, there are no leaves there.   (Hold hands out in front with palms up.)

Jack-o'-Lanterns

Five little jack-o'-lanterns sitting on a gate.
The first one said, "It's getting late."
The second one said, "I hear a noise."
The third one said, "It's only some boys."
The fourth one said, "Let's run, let's run."
The fifth one said, "It's Halloween fun."
Then, oooooo went the wind, and out went the light,
And away ran the jack-o'-lanterns on Halloween night.

(Use as a flannel board poem. Make five pumpkins.)

Four Big Jack-o'-Lanterns

Four big jack-o'-lanterns made a funny sight,
Sitting on a gatepost Halloween night.
Number one said, "I see a witch's hat."
Number two said, "I see a big black cat."
Number three said, "I see a scary ghost."
Number four said, "By that other post."
Four big jack-o'-lanterns weren't a bit afraid.
They marched right along in the Halloween parade.

(Let children take turns acting out this poem.)

Halloween Ghost

There once was a ghost
    (Extend hand and wiggle
    fingers.)
Who lived in a cave.
    (Form hollow with palm for a
    "cave.")
She scared all of the people
    (Point to children.)
And the animals away.
She said, "Boo" to a fox,
    (Point.)
She said, "Boo" to a bee,
    (Point.)
She said, "Boo" to a bear,
    (Point.)
She said "Boo" to me!
    (Point at self.)
Well, she scared that fox,
    (Nod head "yes.")
And she scared that bee.
    (Nod head "yes.")
She scared that bear,
    (Nod head "yes.")
But she didn't scare me!
    (Shake head "no.")

Halloween

Leaves are falling! Leaves are falling!   (Twirl on tiptoe.)
Pumpkins calling! Pumpkins calling!   (Cup hands to mouth.)
Halloween! Halloween!   (Jump high in the air, kick feet together, clap hands over head.)

Witches riding! Witches riding!   (Pretend to gallop on broomstick.)
Goblins hiding! Goblins hiding!   (Crouch down, hide head under arm.)
Halloween! Halloween!   (Jump high in the air, kick feet together, clap hands over head.)

(Beat the rhythm on a drum while children chant the words and act out the poem.)

Little Ghosts

The first little ghost floated by the store.
The second little ghost stood outside the door.
The third little ghost tried her best to hide.
The fourth little ghost stood by my side.
The fifth little ghost near the window sill
Gave everybody a great big thrill.
The five little ghosts were all my friends,
And that is the way this story ends.

(Make puppet ghosts by rolling up a ball of newspaper, laying a large square of white fabric over it, and tying it at the neck. Draw eyes and a mouth with a black marker.)

Here Is the Witch's Tall Black Hat

Here is the witch's tall black hat.
   (Hold arms together over your head.)
Here are the whiskers on her cat.
   (Put together index fingers and thumbs and
   pull back and forth under your nose.)
Here is an owl sitting in a tree.
   (Circle eyes with fingers.)
Here is a goblin! Hee, hee, hee!
   (Hold hands on stomach.)

The Witch

A funny old woman with a pointed cap
   (Hold arms together over your head.)
On my door went rap, rap, rap.
   (Make a knocking motion with fist.)
I was going to the door to see who was there,
   (Swing arms as if you were walking.)
When off on her broomstick she rode through
the air.
   (Sail hand high through the air.)

Three Little Witches

One little, two little, three little witches,
Ride through the sky on a broom.
One little, two little, three little witches,
Wink their eyes at the moon.

(Hold up fingers one by one.)
(Move hand quickly "through the sky.")
(Hold up fingers again.)
(Wink one eye, make circle with arm.)

Little Ghost

I saw a little ghost,
   (Hold hands over eyes.)
And he saw me too!
   (Point to self.)
When I said, "Hi!"
   (wave hand)
He said, "Boo!"
   (Hold hands in front.)

Through the Year

I Am Thankful

I am thankful for pets.
I am thankful for school.
I am thankful when I
Can swim in a pool.
I am thankful for home
And the food that I eat.
I am thankful for all
The new friends that I meet.
I am thankful for health
And for my family.
I'm especially thankful
That I am just ME!

(Ask: "Could anyone in this class have written this poem? Does it say what you might have said about being thankful? Tell us something that you are thankful for, and I will write it on the board. Why are you glad that you are YOU? Did you pronounce the first sound in the word *thankful*? Say the word with me: "thankful." Show me something in this room that you are thankful for.")

Thanksgiving

Mr. Turkey went for a walk
On a bright, sunshiny day.
And on the way he met Mr. Duck,
Gobble, gobble . . . Quack, quack!
And they both went on their way.

(Have children take turns playing the parts of the turkey and the duck.)

The Turkey

A turkey I saw on Thanksgiving,
His tail was spread so wide.
   (Make fist for turkey and spread
   fingers of other hand for tail.)
Shhh . . . don't tell that you've seen him,
   (Make *shhh* sound with index finger to
   lips.)
For he's running away to hide!

Once There Was a Pilgrim

Once there was a pilgrim	(Extend one finger up.)
Who tried every way,	(Nod head.)
To catch a turkey	(Make fist for turkey; spread fingers of other hand for tail.)
For Thanksgiving Day.	
She said, "Caught you!" to the turkey,	(Make catching motion; make "turkey-nod" head motion.)
She said, "Caught you!" to the hen,	(Make a catching motion.)
She said, "Caught you!" to the pumpkin,	(Make a catching motion.)
She said, "Caught you!" to me!	(Point at self.)
Well, she caught that turkey,	(Nod head "yes" and hold arms close to body.)
And she caught that hen.	
She even got the pumpkin,	(Hold hands close to body.)
But she didn't catch me!	(Shake head "no.")

Cute Little Snowman

A cute little snowman
Had a carrot nose.
   (Hold up left fist for snowman.)
Along came a rabbit,
And what do you suppose?
   (Hold up two fingers of right hand for
   rabbit.)
That hungry little rabbit,
Looking for its lunch,
   (Move right hand back and forth.)
Ate that snowman's carrot nose,
Nibble, nibble, crunch!
   (Lightly pinch left fist with right hand.)

Adapted Traditional

Five Snowmen

Five happy snowmen standing in a row.
The sun melted one; it was so very slow.
Four happy snowmen having lots of fun.
One ran indoors to hide from the sun.
Three happy snowmen jumping up and down.
One ran away without a sound.
Two happy snowmen sliding down a hill.
Both fell over and lay very still.

(Use cutouts of five snowmen on craft sticks with this rhyme.)

A Happy, Jolly Fellow

A snowman sits upon the hill.
He's a happy, jolly fellow.
His hat is black, his scarf is red,
And his mittens are bright yellow.

I Am a Snow Person

I am a snow person made of snow.
I stand quite still at ten below,   (Stand tall.)
With a big potato for a nose   (Point to nose.)
And worn out shoes to make my toes.   (Point to feet.)
I have two apples for my eyes   (Point to eyes.)
And a woolen coat about this size.   (Measure.)
I have a muffler warm and red   (Circle neck with hands.)
And a funny hat upon my head.   (Put hands on top of head.)
The sun is coming out. Oh, dear!   (Make circle with arms.)
The sun is melting me I fear.   (Sink slowly to floor.)
Oh, my, I was so nice and round,
Now, I'm just a puddle on the ground!   (Curl up on floor.)

Snowflakes

We are ten little snowflakes   (Move hands in sprinkling motion.)
Floating to the ground.   (Point to ground.)
"*Shhh*," says the fairy,   (Put finger to lips.)
"Do not make a sound."
Children are sleeping,   (Clasp hands behind tilted head.)
But when they open their eyes,   (Point to eyes.)
The lovely white snow
Will be such a surprise.   (Spread hands as if making a blanket.)

Through the Year

Groundhog Day

February second   (Hold up two fingers.)
Is Groundhog Day.
Will he see his shadow,   (Shade eyes with hands.)
And what will he say?
If he says, "More cold,"   (Hug self.)
If he says, "More snow,"   (Raise arms and let fingers wiggle as they fall.)
Then into his hole
He will surely go.   (Hide fist behind back.)

I Have a Shadow

I have a little shadow
    (Point to self.)
Who lives with me.
    (Shake head "yes.")
When the sun comes out,
    (Make circle above head with arms.)
So does he (she)!
    (Nod head "yes.")

Five Little Valentines

Five little valentines were having a race.
The first one was all covered with lace.
The second one had a funny face.
The third one said, "I love you."
The fourth one said, "I do too."
The fifth one was sly as a fox.
He ran the fastest to your valentine box.

(This is a fun rhyme for the flannel board.
Make five hearts. Decorate one with lace;
make one with a funny face, one with a
fox face, and two that say "I love you.")

Special Valentine

(Prepare five valentines and five envelopes to use
on the flannel board or magnetic white board.)

Look at all these valentines.
    (Place valentines on board.)
I made one for each friend.
I'll put them in some envelopes,
    (Place envelopes on board under valentines.)
So each one I can send.
How many valentines do you see?
Start to count them now with me.
One, two, three, four, five.
One for (name of child),
One for _____,
One for _____ too.
One for _____,
And here is one for YOU!
    (Point to child.)

(Repeat until you have said every child's name.)

Five Little Valentines

Five little valentines just for you.
The first one says, "My love is so true."
The second one says, "You have my heart."
The third one says, "Let us never part."
The fourth one says, "Won't you please be mine?"
The fifth one says, "'Til the end of time."

My Little Kite

I have a little kite—the best I've ever seen.
It has a long tail colored white and green.
Dance, little kite! Wiggle and dance!
Along the ground you bounce and prance.
Up in the air my kite starts to go.
Up, up, up, swaying to and fro.
Fly, little kite! Fly and sail!
Dip and dive and shake your tail!
It's fun to fly my little kite.
I hold the string and hold on tight.
If I should let go, away you'd fly.
Good-bye, little kite! Good-bye! Good-bye!

La Mariposa/The Butterfly

Uno, dos, tres, cuatro, cinco,
    (Pop up fingers on right hand as you count.)
Cogi una mariposa de un brinco.
Seis, siete, ocho, nueve, diez,
    (Pop up fingers on left hand as you count.)
La solte brincando otra vez.
One, two, three, four, five,
    (Pop up fingers on right hand as you count.)
I caught a butterfly.
Six, seven, eight, nine, ten.
    (Pop up fingers on left hand as you count.)
I let him go again.

Mother Dear

Mother dear, can you guess
Who it is that loves you best?
I'll give you three guesses—1, 2, 3.
There! I knew you'd think of me!

(This is a nice verse to include in Valentine's
Day cards for the children's mothers.)

Who Has Seen the Wind?

Who has seen the wind?
Neither I nor you;
But when the leaves hang trembling,
The wind is passing through.
Who has seen the wind?
Neither you nor I;
But when the trees bow their heads,
The wind is passing by.

Mother's Day

Five flower baskets sitting on the floor.
One will go to _____'s mom,
Then there will be four.
Four flower baskets, pretty as can be.
One will go to _____'s mom,
Then there will be three.
Three flower baskets with flowers red and
blue.
One will go to _____'s mom,
Then there will be two.
Two flower baskets, bright as the sun.
One will go to _____'s mom,
Then there will be one.
One flower basket, oh, it's sure to go
To your very own mother, who is the
Nicest one you know.

(Make five flower baskets for the flannel
board to use with this rhyme.)

Through the Year

Birds and Spring

I am a bird all dressed in black.
I flew away, but now I've come back.
I am a bird all dressed in blue.
I like to fly, and I like to sing too.
I am a bird all dressed in green.
I am the smallest bird ever seen.
I am a bird; I am in orange you know.
Whenever I fly, you can see me glow.
Four birds fly and four birds sing.
They all seem to know that now it is spring.

(Show pictures of birds the children have learned.)

Birds

Here is a tall, straight tree.
   (Stand.)
Here are five birds you can see.
   (Wiggle five fingers.)
One, two, three, four, five to arrive!
   (Bend down fingers.)
Now, let's count again to five.
   (Repeat action.)

Flower

I'd like to be a flower
   (Cup hands together.)
With petals for my head.
When nighttime comes,
I'd fold up
   (Fold hands together.)
And never go to bed.
   (Shake head "no.")

The Little Bird

Once I saw a little bird
   (Extend left arm and index finger.)
Go hop, hop, hop.
   (Extend middle finger of right hand; make fingers "hop.")
So I said, "Little bird,
Will you stop, stop, stop?"
   (Hold palm out as if a police officer.)
I went to the window
To say, "How do you do?"
But, she shook her head,
   (Shake head "no.")
And away she flew.
   (Flap arms to the sides.)

My Garden

This is my garden;
I'll rake it with care,
And then some flower seeds,
I'll plant in there.
The sun will shine,
And the rain will fall,
And my garden will blossom,
And grow straight and tall.

(Extend one hand, palm up.)
("Rake" with three fingers of other hand.)
(Make planting motion with fingers.)

(Make circle above head with hands.)
(Flutter fingers for rain.)
(Cup hands together, extending upward.)

Through the Year

American Flag

As red as a fire,
As blue as the sky,
As white as the snow
See the flag fly!
Three pretty colors
Wave at the sky.
Red, white, and blue
On the Fourth of July!
Red, white, and blue
Those colors are,
And every state
Has its very own star.
Hold up the flag.
Hold it up high,
And then say, "Hurrah,
For the Fourth of July!"

(Discuss the U.S. states. Ask: "How many
stars are on the flag? What do the stars
stand for? Can you draw a flag?")

A Seashell

One day a little shell washed up
  (Hold shell.)
Out of the waves at sea.
I held the shell up to my ear,
  (Hold shell to ear.)
And I heard it sing to me.
Sh, sh, sh, sh.
  (Children repeat.)
A little shell washed up one day
And lay upon the sand.
  (Hold shell in hand.)
It sang a song about the sea,
As I held it in my hand.
Sh, sh, sh, sh.
  (Children repeat.)

(This is excellent for practicing the /sh/ sound. Bring in
a conch shell and let children take turns holding it to
their ears to hear the sound of the sea.)

At the Seashore

Down at the seashore,
Isn't it grand?
Wiggling my toes   (Wiggle toes.)
In the soft, warm sand.
Building a tall sand castle   (Make building motions.)
Where the king and queen can stay,
But when the tide comes rushing in   (Sweep one arm inward.)
They will have to move away!   (Make leveling motion with arm.)
Splashing in the water   (Make splashing motions with hands.)
Of the cool blue sea,
Playing wave tag, in and out,   (Run forward with small steps.)
You can't catch me!   (Run backward quickly.)
Holding up a seashell   (Hold fist tightly to ear.)
Tightly to my ear.
Shh! It's telling me a secret   (Hold finger to lips with other hand.)
That only I can hear!

Animals

Monkey See, Monkey Do

A little monkey likes to do
Just the same as you and you.
When you sit up very tall,
Monkey sits up very tall.
When you pretend to throw a ball,
Monkey pretends to throw a ball.
When you try to touch your toes,
Monkey tries to touch his toes.
When you move your little nose,
Monkey moves his little nose.
When you jump up in the air,
Monkey jumps up in the air.
When you sit down in a chair,
Monkey sits down in a chair.

(Continue this game using other movements, rhyming, or otherwise. Use this action game to precede a rest time or as a readiness activity.)

At the Zoo

One, two, three. What did I see at the zoo?
One, two, three. Guess when I give you a clue.
I saw an animal with a long neck. (giraffe)
I saw the king of beasts that gives a loud roar. (lion)
I saw a large animal with a long trunk. (elephant)
I saw a big cat with orange and black stripes. (tiger)
I saw a big, furry animal that hibernates in winter. (bear)
One, two, three. What do you see at the zoo?
One, two, three. Give us a clue. We'll guess who.

(Give each child the opportunity to give a clue.)

Rhinoceros

A rhinoceros, a rhinoceros,
Sometimes he makes a dreadful fuss.
He has a big horn on his nose.   (Extend index finger from nose.)
He snorts and rumbles as he goes.   (Have children say "Grump!")
He's very long and very wide.   (Measure length and width with hands.)
He has a very wrinkled hide.   (Make wavy motion with hands.)
He has big hooves on his four feet.   (Hold up four fingers.)
We feed him grass and hay to eat.
A rhinoceros, a rhinoceros,
Is surely not a pet for us.   (Shake head "no.")

(Show a picture of a rhinoceros. Write the rhyme on a chart. Ask: "Why wouldn't a rhinoceros make a good pet?")

Animals

Hoppity Toad

I am a funny hoppity toad
   (Squat down.)
Trying to jump across the road.
   (Jump in squatting position.)
Winking, blinking my big eyes,
   (Blink eyes.)
Snapping at some bugs and flies.
   (Open and close mouth quickly.)

The Squirrel

Sneaky, squeaky
Hippity, hop.   (Hop.)
Up he goes   (Stretch arms up.)
To the tree top.
Whirly, twirly   (Spin around.)
Round and round.
Down he scampers   (Sit down.)
To the ground.

Frog

"*Croak*," said the frog   (Make croaking sound.)
With his golden eyes.   (Hold fists up to eyes.)
Sitting on a lily pad,
Catching flies.   (Grab air with hand.)
I have a sticky tongue;   (Make darting motion with index finger.)
It's as fast as can be.
I catch the mosquitoes,
one, two three.

(Use as a flannel board rhyme.)

Houses

This is a nest for the bluebird.
   (Cup hands and hold palms up.)
This is a hive for the bee.
   (Hold fists together, palm to palm.)
This is a hole for the bunny rabbit,
   (Make a hole with fingers.)
And this is a house for me.
   (Hold fingertips together to make a peak.)

Two Little Squirrels

Two little squirrels
Were scampering through the wood.
Two little squirrels
Were looking for food.
Bushy Tail found two nuts.
Bright Eyes found two more.
How many nuts were there
For their winter store?

Animals

Hop and Stop

The first little rabbit went hop, hop, hop.
I said to the first rabbit, "Stop, stop, stop!"
The second little rabbit went run, run, run.
I said to the second rabbit, "Fun, fun, fun!"
The third little rabbit went thump, thump, thump.
I said to the third rabbit, "Jump, jump, jump!"
The fourth little rabbit went sniff, sniff, snuff.
I said to the fourth rabbit, "That is enough!"
The fifth little rabbit went creep, creep, creep.
I said to the fifth rabbit, "It's time to sleep!"

(Because words repeat, the children should be able
to say the entire rhyme with you the second time.)

I Saw a Rabbit

I saw a rabbit.	(Put hand over eyes.)
I said, "Hi."	(Point to self and wave "hi.")
He didn't stop.	(Shake head "no.")
He went on by.	
Hop, hop, hop.	(Make two fingers "hop.")

Squirrel

Whirly, twirly
    (Twirl index fingers around each other.)
Look at the squirrel
Sitting in the tree,
Stuffing nuts in her cheeks,
    (Puff up cheeks.)
One, two, three.

Rabbits

A family of rabbits lived under a tree,	(Close right hand and hide it under left arm.)
A father, a mother, and babies three.	(Hold up thumb and then fingers in succession.)
Sometimes the bunnies would sleep all day,	(Make a fist.)
But when night came they liked to play.	(Wiggle fingers.)
Out of the hole they'd go creep, creep, creep	(Move fingers in creeping motion.)
While the birds in the trees were all asleep.	(Rest face on hands, placing palms together.)
Then, the bunnies would scamper about and run,	(Wiggle fingers.)
Uphill, downhill! Oh, what fun!	(Move fingers vigorously.)
But, when Mother said, "It's time to rest."	(Hold up index finger.)
Pop! They would hurry	(Clap hands after "Pop!")
Right back to their nest!	(Hide hand under arm.)

Pets

What Animals Do

We'll hop, hop, hop like a bunny.
And run, run, run like a dog.
We'll walk, walk, walk like an elephant
And jump, jump, jump like a frog.
We'll swim, swim, swim like a goldfish
And fly, fly, fly like a bird.
We'll sit right down and fold our hands
And not say a single word.

There Was a Little Turtle

There was a little turtle;
    (Make small circle with hands.)
He lived in a box.
    (Make a box with hands.)
He swam in a puddle.
    (Wiggle hands.)
He climbed on the rocks.
    (Climb fingers of one hand up over other.)
He snapped at a mosquito.
    (Clap hands.)
He snapped at a flea.
    (Clap hands.)
He snapped at a minnow.
    (Clap hands.)
He snapped at me.
    (Point to self.)
He caught a mosquito.
    (Hold fingers up, snapping them shut.)
He caught the flea.
    (Repeat above.)
He caught the minnow,
    (Repeat above.)
But he didn't catch me.
    (Bend fingers only halfway.)

Pets in Our Classroom

One white rabbit came to our classroom,
And she stayed only one day.
We fed her lettuce and carrots.
It's too bad she couldn't stay.
Two hamsters came to our classroom.
They filled their little cheeks
With vegetables and lots of fruit,
And they made sharp little squeaks.
Three caterpillars came to our classroom.
They stayed, but by and by,
One day we went to look at them,
Each was a butterfly!
Four canaries came to our classroom,
And for us they did sing.
They made great entertainment
As we watched them swing.
Five fish came to our classroom.
They were quite a lively brood.
We liked to watch them swim around
And dart up for their food.
Six turtles came to our classroom,
In a terrarium.
It had warm water and a rock.
Good pets they did become.
Seven lizards came to our classroom.
They needed a terrarium too.
They ate all kinds of insects
And gave us quite a view.
Eight red ants came to our classroom,
In a box of glass.
We fed them drops of honey.
They were fun to have in class.
So, we have had some visitors,
And each one was a pet.
If you could have a choice of them,
Which one would you get?

(Have children hold up the designated
number of fingers. Pause for a discussion
about each animal, bird, or insect.)

Pets

Turtles

One little turtle feeling so blue;   (Hold up one finger.)
Along came another. Now, there are two.   (Hold up two fingers.)
Two little turtles on their way to tea;
Along came another. Now, there are three. (Hold up three fingers.)
Three little turtles going to the store;
Along came another. Now, there are four.   (Hold up four fingers.)
Four little turtles going for a drive;
Along came another. Now, there are five.   (Hold up five fingers.)

Goldfish Pets

One little goldfish lived in a bowl.
Two little goldfish eat their food whole.
Three little goldfish swim all around.
Although they move, they don't make a sound.
Four little goldfish have swishy tails.
Five little goldfish have pretty scales.

(Have children cut fish from yellow construction paper and lay them on the flannel board. If the board is slanted slightly backward, the fish will cling. Children may add one fish at a time and count as they do so.)

My Pets

There are lots of pets in my house.
I have one gerbil and one white mouse.
    (Hold up one finger on each hand.)
I have two kittens and two green frogs.
    (Hold up two fingers on each hand.)
I have three goldfish and three big dogs.
    (Hold up three fingers on each hand.)
Some folks say that is a lot!
Can you tell how many pets I've got?
    (12)

Five Little Puppies

Five little puppies were playing in the sun;   (Hold up hand, fingers extended.)
This one saw a rabbit, and he began to run.   (Bend down first finger.)
This one saw a butterfly, and she began to race;   (Bend down second finger.)
This one saw a pussy cat, and he began to chase;   (Bend down third finger.)
This one tried to catch her tail, and she went round and round;   (Bend down fourth finger.)
This one was so quiet, he never made a sound.   (Bend down thumb.)

The Little Mouse

There was a little mouse   (Hold up fist.)
Who lived in his house.   (Cover fist with opposite palm.)
He wiggled his ears,   (Wiggle fist.)
He wiggled his nose;   (Wiggle nose.)
Then, he wiggled his toes!   (Point to toes.)
He crept toward the dog,   (Creep fingers.)
He crept toward the cat,   (Creep fingers.)
He even crept toward me!   (Point to self.)
He stared at the dog,   (Stare, wide-eyed.)
He stared at the cat,   (Stare, wide-eyed.)
But he just wiggled and giggled   (Wiggle, smile, giggle.)
When he got to me!   (Point to self.)

Things that Crawl, Creep, and Fly

Four Little Owls

This little owl has great round eyes.
This little owl is of very small size.
This little owl can turn her head.
This little owl likes mice, she said.
This little owl flies all around,
And her wings make hardly a single sound.

(Pretend a desk or table is the tree. Have one child be the owl and another the sun. The owl sleeps. The sun goes down. The owl awakens and flies away to look for food for her babies. The sun comes up, and the owl goes back to her tree.)

The Fuzzy Little Caterpillar

The fuzzy little caterpillar
Curled up on a leaf,
    (Make self small.)
Spun her little chrysalis,
And then fell fast asleep.
    (Rest cheek on folded hands.)
While she was sleeping,
She dreamed that she could fly,
    (Smile.)
And later when she woke up,
She was a butterfly!
    (Pretend to fly around room.)

Elizabeth McKinnon

Tap, Tap, Tap

Tap, tap, tap goes the woodpecker   (Tap with right index finger on inside of left wrist.)
As he pecks a hole in a tree.   (Make circle with index finger and thumb.)
He is making a house with a window
To peep at you and me.   (Hold circle made with index finger and thumb in front of eye.)

The Beehive

Here is the beehive;
    (Make a fist.)
Where are the bees?
    (Tilt head to one side.)
Hidden inside where nobody sees.
Here they come buzzing out of the hive,
    (Slowly begin to open fist.)
One, two, three, four, and five!
    (Raise fingers one at a time.)

Adapted Traditional

Rocket Ship

Our rocket ship is standing by,
    (Hold up one finger.)
And very, very soon,
We'll have a countdown, then we'll blast
Ourselves up to the moon.
Begin to count: ten, nine, eight,
    (Hold up 10 fingers; then, count backward,
    bending down each finger.)
Be on time, don't be late.
Seven, six, five, and four,
There aren't many seconds more.
Three, two, one! Zero! Zip!
The rocket is off on its first moon trip.

Bumblebee

I'm a little bumblebee; watch me go   (Place index finger on arm; then, fly it upward.)
Buzz, buzz, buzz, buzz, to and fro.   (Fly finger back and forth.)
When I find a flower blooming nearby,   (Fly finger down into cupped hand.)
I drink its nectar and away I fly.   (Fly finger up and away.)

Weather

Clouds

The clouds are floating through the sky.	(Hold hands up high and move them in floating motion.)
They seem to wave as they go by.	(Wave hands.)
Some shaped like animals I know.	(Make odd shapes with arms and hands.)
Some look like pretty drifts of snow.	(Move hands across front in drifting motion.)

The Rain

Pitter-patter raindrops
Falling from the sky.
　(Wiggle fingers to imitate falling rain.)
Here is my umbrella
To keep me safe and dry!
　(Raise hands over your head.)
When the rain is over,
And the sun begins to glow,
　(Make a large circle with arms.)
Little flowers start to bud
And grow and grow and grow.
　(Spread hands apart slowly.)

Two Little Rabbits

Two little rabbits hopped to the gate.
　(Make two fingers "hop.")
Two little rabbits ate and ate.
　(Make eating motions.)
Soon, they heard a noise
That sounded like thunder,
　(Clap hands.)
And when they reached that gate,
They hopped right under!
　(Make two fingers "dive" downward.)

Fun in the Rain

When rain comes down,
Drip, drop, drip, drop.
(Flutter fingers.)
Windshield wipers
Flip, flop, flip, flop,
(Move forearm back and forth.)
And boots in puddles,
Plip, plop, plip, plop.
(Pretend to splash in a puddle.)
I wish the rain would never stop.
Drip, drop, drip,
(Repeat all motions.)
Flip, flop, flip,
Plip, plop, plip, plop, PLOP!

(Jump with both feet on final PLOP.)

The Rabbit

I have a little rabbit.
　(Make fist, thumb on top.)
He lives in a tree.
When the sun comes out,
So does he!
　(Pop thumb up.)

The Wind

The wind came out to play one day.	(Make sweeping motions with arms.)
He (she) swept the clouds out of his (her) way.	(Make fluttering motions with fingers.)
He (she) blew the leaves and away they flew.	(Lift arms and lower them.)
The trees bent low, and their branches did too.	(Repeat sweeping motions.)
The wind blew the great big ships at sea.	
The wind blew my kite away from me.	

A Farmer

If I were a farmer
(Point to self.)
With flour, milk, and meat,
I'd sell you these and other things
That you would like to eat.
(Make eating motion.)

(Make a chart with children listing all of the foods that are grown on a farm.)

Painting

Paint the ceiling, paint the door,
Paint the walls, and paint the floor.
Paint the roof—slush, slush, slush!
Paint the doorstep with your brush.
Now, my house is done, you see.
You may come and visit me.
I've been working very hard
To paint my playhouse in the yard.

(Pantomime the action of painting. Ask, "What else would you paint if you were painting a house?")

Different People

This person drives a taxi.
This person leads a band.
This person guides the traffic
By holding up a hand.
This person brings the letters.
This person rakes and hoes.
This person is a funny clown
Who dances on tiptoes.

(Invite children to choose which person they might like to be, pantomime the action, and name the worker. Ask them to use no words but only hands, feet, and bodies. Ask, "Did we leave out anyone? Who? Shall we add the worker to the poem?")

Our Community Helpers

Some people bring us produce
And drinks all fresh and cold.
Some people work in shops and stores
Where many things are sold.
Some people bring us letters,
And they take more mail away.
Some people stop the traffic
To help us on our way.
Some people move our furniture
And put it in a van.
Some people take the garbage
And empty every can.

(Ask children what some other people do to help us. "What does a weather person do? What does a sailor who goes to sea do?" Let them choose the helpers they might like to be when they grow up.)

Farm Animals (response)

Listen to the riddle and you can name
A farm animal when you play this game.
At night my home's a stable. It keeps out the rain.
My baby is a foal. I eat lots of grass and grain. (horse)
I live in a coop and have two legs.
I have feathers. You eat my eggs. (chicken)
I live on a farm. I have four feet.
My baby is a calf. I provide milk so sweet. (cow)
I help the farmer by catching mice.
I have fur. The farmer treats me nice. (cat)
I stay in a fold at night on the farm.
My coat will keep you very warm. (sheep)
I help the farmer bring in the cows.
Sometimes the farmer takes me into her house. (dog)
On the farm, I stay in a pen.
I play in the mud and oink with my friends. (pig)

How We Travel

Around and About

Around and about, around and about.
   (Do actions as rhyme indicates.)
Over and under and in and out.
Run through a field, swim in the sea.
Slide down a hill, climb up a tree.

My Bicycle

One wheel, two wheels on the ground;
   (Revolve hand in forward circle to form a wheel.)
My feet make the pedals go round and round.
   (Move feet in pedaling motion.)
Handlebars help me steer so straight
   (Pretend to steer a bicycle.)
Down the sidewalk and through the gate.

Magic Feet

Have you seen my magic feet
   (Do actions as rhyme indicates.)
Dancing down the magic street?
Sometimes fast, sometimes slow,
Sometimes high, sometimes low.

Come and dance along with me.
Dance just like my feet you see.
First, we'll slide and then we'll hop;
Then, we'll spin and then we'll stop.

Let's Ride the Bumps

Let's ride the bumps as we drive in the car.
   (Bounce up and down in chair.)
Now let's stand and touch a star.
   (Stand and reach high.)
Let's be jumping jacks, and then
   (Jump.)
Let's be still and sit down again.
   (Sit.)

Adapted Traditional

Choo-Choo Train

This is a choo-choo train,   (Bend arms at elbows.)
Puffing down the track.   (Rotate forearms in rhythm.)
Now it's going forward,   (Push arms forward; continue rotating motion.)
Now it's going back.   (Pull arms back; continue rotating motion.)
Now the bell is ringing.   (Pull bell cord with closed fist.)
Now the whistle blows.   (Hold fist near mouth and say, "*Toot, toot.*")
What a lot of noise it makes   (Cover ears with hands.)
Everywhere it goes.   (Stretch out arms.)

The Airplane

The airplane has big wide wings.   (Stretch out arms.)
Its propeller spins around and sings.   (Make one arm go around.)
Vvvvvvv!   (Make the sound.)
The airplane goes up in the sky.   (Lift arms up and then down.)
Then down it goes, just see it fly!
Vvvvvvv!   (Make the sound.)
Up, up, and up; down, down, and down;   (Make continuous up and down movements.)
Over every housetop in our town.
Vvvvvvv!   (Make the sound.)

I'm a Special Person!

Materials: craft paper roll, ribbon, fabric samples, yarn

All children can work together to celebrate a special person for "Child of the Week," a birthday, or another special occasion. On a large sheet of craft paper, trace an outline of the special child. Ask children to work together to turn the drawing into a likeness of the child. Does she often wear a bow in her hair? If so, have one child cut out a fabric bow and attach it to the drawing. Does she have brown eyes? Allow another child to color or paint them on. Does she like to read? Have another make a paper book to attach to the hand of the drawing. As each child contributes something, the special child will feel unique and confident.

Sticky Mural

Materials: clear, self-stick paper (sold in rolls in discount stores); collage materials

Working together to create a finished product will instill pride in each child. Cut a 6-foot (1.8-m) length from a roll of clear, self-stick paper. Carefully remove the backing. Tape the self-stick paper to a wall with the sticky side out. Collect a variety of lightweight collage materials, such as ribbons, feathers, sequins, small fabric scraps, and paper scraps. Have children sit by the sticky paper. Show them how the collage materials stick to the paper. Let them come up and touch the paper if they would like. Then, let children take turns adding collage materials to the sticky paper until it is completely covered.

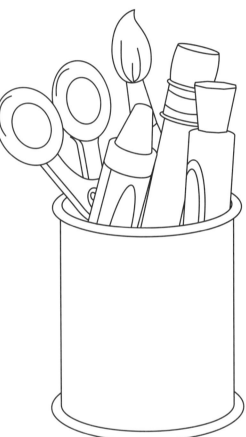

Brick Building Mural

Materials: red construction paper, butcher or craft roll paper

Fold sheets of red construction paper in thirds. Hang a length of butcher or craft roll paper on a wall at children's eye level. Give each child a sheet of folded construction paper. Show children how to cut their papers along the folds to make construction paper "bricks." For younger children, precut the paper brick shapes and place rolls of tape on the backs of them. Distribute the paper bricks to children one at a time. Let children work together taping or gluing the bricks to the butcher paper to build a house, a fort, or a wall. While they are working, sing the first two verses of the following song. When they are finished, have them tell you the name of their creation. Substitute that name for the word *building* in the last verse of the song.

Sing to the tune of: "Here We Go 'Round the Mulberry Bush."

Brick by brick we'll build it up,
Build it up, build it up.
Brick by brick we'll build it up.
We'll build it up so high.
Brick by brick we'll work together,
Work together, work together.
Brick by brick we'll work together.
We'll work together fine.
Brick by brick we built a building,
Built a building, built a building.
Brick by brick we built a building.
We built a building today.

Gayle Bittinger

Weaving Net

Materials: sports net, string or ribbon, 2 chairs, weaving materials

Children will enjoy the variations of this fine motor group activity. Use a durable but no longer used sports net (volleyball, badminton, etc.) or hammock for this activity. Tie the net to two sturdy chairs (ones that will not tip over if the net is pulled or pushed). Position the chairs so that the net is spread out. Collect a variety of weaving materials as suggested below. Have children sit around the net. Using a length of string or ribbon, show them how to weave it in and out of the holes in the net. Let the children use the weaving materials to weave horizontal, vertical, and diagonal patterns across the net. Encourage them to work together to create their own weaving designs. Hang the children's completed weaving on a wall or a bulletin board.

Nature Weaving: Take children on a nature walk to collect items for weaving. For example, children could use small twigs, leaves, flowers, and long blades of grass in their weaving.

Ribbon Weaving: Cut colorful ribbons into a variety of lengths. Let the children weave the ribbons throughout the net. To make it a little more challenging, have children weave the ribbons in a color pattern such as red-yellow-green-red-yellow-green.

Paper Weaving: Set out various kinds of paper, such as construction paper, wrapping paper, newspaper, and brown paper bags. Help children cut the papers into strips that can be woven into the net. If needed, tape the strips together to make them long enough for weaving.

 (See page 2.)

Nature Mural

Materials: nature walk objects such as leaves, twigs, seeds; large peeled crayons; butcher or craft roll paper (Light colors work best.); masking tape

Children love the idea of outdoor circle time. Start this activity with a group walk through the playground or other safe outdoor area. Have children collect objects that interest them: crunchy leaves during autumn or seed pods in the spring. Secure the objects to a patio or other flat surface with rolled pieces of tape on the back of each. Place a large sheet of craft paper over the nature objects and weigh or tape the paper down. Have children sit around the paper and feel the nature objects under the paper. Then, have each child choose a crayon and rub gently over the spot on the paper above his nature object to create a colorful rubbing. The overall effect of the nature mural will make a dazzling spring or autumn art display.

 (See page 2.)

Chalk It Up

Materials: colorful chalk, butcher or craft roll paper (Dark colors work best.), small scraps of construction paper, masking tape

The final chalk product will bring smiles of surprise to the children. Tape a large sheet of butcher or craft paper to a patio or other flat surface. Have children spread the construction paper scraps in different spots across the large background paper. Tape the construction paper to the large paper with rolled pieces of tape on the back of each. Have each child choose a piece of chalk and completely color a section of the large paper, coloring the construction paper pieces and all of the surrounding large paper. When complete, remove the construction paper scraps to reveal the paper beneath.

Caterpillar to Butterfly

Young children are naturally imaginative and playful. Encourage their imaginations with a lot of dramatic play during circle time. Let children pretend that they are caterpillars in cocoons, waiting to become butterflies. How would it feel to be wrapped up in a cocoon? What might it be like to know that your body is changing, and you will wake up as something else? Have each child slowly change into a butterfly and fly around the room meeting other butterflies.

Tadpole to Frog

Designate the circle as a little pond. Encourage children to pretend that they are tadpoles swimming in the water. Have them keep their arms at their sides and their legs together for a tail. Now, have them slowly turn into frogs. First, they will grow one hind leg and then grow the other hind leg. Do the same with the front legs (arms). Let the new frogs jump about. Ask them, "How does it feel to have legs to hop on? What is it like to be able to move out of the water onto dry land?" Gather all of the frogs around the edge of the pond. Have them sit and croak. Then, pretend to be a child hunting for pet frogs and have the children jump into the pond as you approach.

Row Your Boat

Materials: masking tape; dramatic play props such as hats, binoculars, and life jackets; long cardboard tubes

Children will enjoy the music and movement of this activity. Ask children to sit on the floor in pairs. As they sit, have each pair of children face each other, hold hands, and touch feet. Have them gently rock forward and backward while singing, "Row, Row, Row Your Boat."

> *Sing to the tune of: "Row, Row, Row Your Boat"*
>
> Waves, waves, back and forth,
> Rock the boat all day.
> We row and row so we can go
> Somewhere far away.
>
> *Jean Warren*

Use masking tape to make a boat outline on the floor. Provide hats, binoculars, life jackets, and long cardboard tube "oars." Encourage children to take imaginary journeys to places near or far in their boat. Then, sing the following song, substituting the name of the children's destination for the word *island*.

> *Sing to the tune of: "My Bonnie Lies over the Ocean."*
>
> We're rowing our boat to the island.
> We're rowing our boat, can't you see?
> We're rowing our boat to the island.
> We're rowing as fast as can be.
> Rowing, rowing, we're rowing our boat.
> Can't you see, you see?
> Rowing, rowing, we're rowing our boat.
> Can't you see?
>
> *Gayle Bittinger*

Nursery Rhyme Fun

Nursery rhymes provide great material for dramatic play. Let children act out these or any other nursery rhymes:

Jumping Tricks

Cut candle and stick shapes from construction paper and tape them 1½ feet (0.46 m) apart on the floor. Encourage children to jump over the candle and stick shapes. If you wish, substitute other items for candles and sticks.

Jack (or Jan) Be Nimble: Set up a small, unlit candle in a candleholder. Let children take turns jumping over the candlestick while they pretend to be Jack or Jan.

Mary (or Marcus) Had a Little Lamb: Choose one child to be Mary or Marcus. Have the other children pretend to be lambs and follow her or him around the room.

Little Miss (or Mister) Muffet: Children love acting out this nursery rhyme. Set a stool in the middle of the circle. Choose one child to sit on the stool and pretend to be Miss or Mister Muffet. Have the child pretend to eat and then run away when you dangle a plastic spider beside her or him.

Follow the Path

On the floor in one part of the room, use masking tape to make a long dashed line. Give each child a turn to try hopping along the line without touching any of the breaks. The children could pretend that they are searching for Bo Peep's lost sheep on the path that the sheep followed.

Bo Peep and the Lost Sheep

This is a revised version of "Hide and Seek." One child is "it" or Bo Peep, and the rest of the children are the lost sheep. Have Bo Peep hide her eyes, and have the "sheep" run and hide. Bo Peep must find as many of the sheep as she can within a time period you set. Let each child have a turn playing Bo Peep (boys included).

Jack and Jill Mat Rolling

Place gymnastics mats on the floor if you have them or use a carpeted floor. Let children pantomime the nursery rhyme "Jack and Jill." Encourage children to practice many different ways to roll: forward rolls, backward rolls, somersaults, sideways rolls, etc.

Mother Goose Activities

Character Poster Masks
Materials: Poster board

Poster masks are wonderful for language development. Young children have so much fun pretending and making up their own stories when they are playing with the masks. This activity takes an extra amount of work on your part, but it is well worth it! Once you have made the Mother Goose character poster masks, you will be able to use them for years to come, and you will save money by making them yourself.

Outline the main character for each Mother Goose rhyme on a large sheet of cardboard or poster board and make holes for the child's face and hands. Next, have children color the characters with crayons or paint.

To use the masks, have one child wear a poster mask with her face and hands showing through the holes. Have the remaining children recite the rhyme as the child wearing the mask acts it out.

Mother Goose Drama
Materials: Mother Goose props

Keep a collection of small objects that relate in some manner to Mother Goose rhymes. For example, you could have a tiny pie for "Little Jack Horner" or "Four and Twenty Blackbirds," a toy sheep for "Bo Peep" and "Little Boy Blue," or a small pail for "Jack and Jill." Have each child choose an object and recite the nursery rhyme while role-playing the character.

Hard-Boiled Humpty Dumpty
Teach children the rhyme "Humpty Dumpty." Give each child a cooled hard-boiled egg. Then, let each child draw Humpty Dumpty's face on his egg and then crack the egg. The children will really be able to see that when Humpty Dumpty cracks, no one will be able to put him back together again. Let children take the eggs home to eat or eat them during snack time.

 (See page 2.)

Farmer in the Dell

This would be a good activity to use before talking about feelings. Choose one child to be the farmer and have him stand in the middle of the circle. Then, sing the song "The Farmer in the Dell." Have children act out the verses by choosing a partner to stand inside the circle with them. On the last verse, have the paired children return to the edge of the circle so that the cheese will be left all alone. Talk about what it was like to be chosen or not to be chosen. How did it feel to be left alone as the cheese?

The Farmer in the Dell

The farmer in the dell,
The farmer in the dell,
Heigh-ho, the derry-o,
The farmer in the dell.

Adapted Traditional

Additional verses: The farmer takes a wife; The wife takes a child; The child takes a dog; The dog takes a cat; The cat takes a rat; The rat takes the cheese; The cheese stands alone.

Pumpkin Patch

This activity would fit into an autumn unit on pumpkins, harvest time, or life on a farm. Choose two or three children to be farmers. Have the remaining children join hands to form a long, winding pumpkin vine. Ask every second or third child on the vine to become a pumpkin. Have the pumpkins crouch down and hug their knees. At your signal, have the farmers "pull" the pumpkins off the vine by gently rolling them over onto their sides. Then, have the pumpkins roll away. Repeat until every child has had a turn being a pumpkin and a farmer.

Earthworms

Bring a clear plastic container filled with earthworms to the circle. Explain that as earthworms dig their way through the soil, they loosen and soften it, which helps plants grow. Spread layers of blankets in the middle of the circle and have children pretend that the blankets are soil. Can they wiggle like worms across the floor?

Did You Ever See an Earthworm?
Sing to the tune of: "Did You Ever See a Lassie?"

Did you ever see an earthworm,
An earthworm, an earthworm?
Did you ever see an earthworm
Move this way and that?
Move this way and that way
And this way and that way.
Did you ever see an earthworm
Move this way and that?

Betty Silkunas

Tunneling

Worms live in the many tunnels they dig in the ground. Talk about what it would be like to live underground. Would you miss the sun? Fresh air? Then, have children stand and form a line. Ask them to stand with their legs apart to form a long tunnel. Tell them that the tunnel ends above ground. One by one, let each child pretend to be a tunneling worm and crawl through everyone's legs. Invite each child to show you what it might be like to come from such a dark place into light.

CD-104452

Circle Time Activities turns circle time into optimum learning time. These child-tested activities foster social and emotional development and extend basic math, problem solving, language, and music, movement, and literacy skills. A concept and activity matrix is included to help early childhood educators identify, focus on, assess, and enhance specific skills for each young learner.

U.S. $12.95

ISBN-13: 978-1-936024-83-4

carsondellosa.com

MADE IN THE USA

EAN